Girls, Rise Up and Shine!

Practical Ways to Achieve Abundant Success and Live Up to Your Full Potential

Table of Contents

Introduction

Young women often struggle with finding a work-life balance. One of the reasons for this is because they are burdened with multiple responsibilities from a young age. They are repeatedly told and conditioned to be warm and caring. Unlike their male counterparts, who are automatically seen as the ones assuming leadership roles. In such instances, an ambitious woman is viewed as being intimidating instead of inspiring.

Women commonly face several challenges and most of them are associated with their gender. Being born as a woman automatically comes with its own set of expectations that are endless and even impossible to a certain extent. They are told what they should do and should be instead of encouraged to live the life they want. When a woman doesn't want to fit the societal mold, she is labeled as an outcast. A man who is chasing his ambitions is seen as a go-getter, while a woman is viewed as selfish because she doesn't want to fit the societal mold of what a woman should be like. Overcoming such biases and stereotypes is overwhelming by itself. Unfortunately, all women face these biases and stereotypes at one point or another. Whether it is in their personal or professional life, no woman is exempt.

Regardless of how far a woman comes in her career, unfortunately, her personal life is the one thing that's always scrutinized. Women are expected to be naturally nurturing, warm, and caring. Why should you always be the nurturer and the giver? Men and women are supposed to be equal and it is high time that we, as a society, accept this truth.

This book will act as your practical guide to help you get through different circumstances in life. It will teach you to let go of self-doubt and instead, imbibe an attitude of positivity. It is filled with practical tips and advice you can use to live a happy and fulfilling life. It will also teach you how to start believing in yourself, work on improving yourself, and improving your self-confidence. By letting go of certain behaviors that are preventing you from growing, you can achieve the impossible. You are not alone on this journey because this book will be your friend and mentor along the way.

Regardless of how bad a circumstance might seem, there is always a way out. It might be difficult to see it immediately, but achieving meaningful success is doable. You can live a life you desire without letting others regulate your dreams and aspirations. You can transform the impossible into possible by changing your attitude and mindset. By letting go of negative beliefs and replacing them with positivity, you can move ahead. You will learn to take positive strides toward living a fulfilling life. You can transform yourself and live up to your full potential by following this advice.

Apart from this, this book will also teach you how to take care of yourself on this journey toward success. You will discover the secrets to dealing with failure and rising up to challenges. You will learn how to prevent any challenges that come your way from paralyzing you by turning them into an advantage. You will learn to face your fears. You will go from being undervalued, to unstoppable and truly extraordinary. Once you learn to stop underestimating your capabilities, you will live like a champion as intended!

Are you wondering how I know all this? Well, I suppose a little introduction is needed! Hello, my name is Nina Young. I know all this because like you, I used to be a girl riddled with self-doubt. Through my own experience, I realized the dire need for young women and working moms to overcome their self-doubt. This is especially true when they are facing challenges while pursuing their dreams. Self-doubt often prevents them from achieving or even realizing their full potential. Most are scared to dream big because they are worried about failing or not fitting the societal mold of what others expect. Once I managed to overcome my self-doubt, understood my true self, and started dreaming big, I realized my potential. I realized I didn't have to settle for what others thought was good enough. Instead, I wanted to do the impossible. I wanted to create a life; a future that I desired. It wasn't just about making it big in my profession, I wanted this happiness in my personal life too.

As a mother of twin girls, I know the different challenges women face daily. As a young girl, I know how difficult it can be to overcome the self-doubt that prevents you from working toward your dreams. My doctoral degree in education coupled with my personal experiences have given me invaluable insight about getting past challenging circumstances and achieving success and inner happiness. I started sharing my tips and suggestions with friends, loved ones, and colleagues. While doing this, I realized the difference simple suggestions can make. That is when I concluded that this advice shouldn't be restricted to a few people, but should be shared with everyone.

Through this book, I want to help prepare you for the different challenges you will face in life. Regardless of whether you are entering the work arena, are already working, or a young mom, I have got your back. There will be different challenges you will need to face in your work and personal life. Learning to overcome these challenges without letting them paralyze you and create self-doubt is important. I hope I will help you learn what I wish I knew when I faced those challenging times. Through conscious living and questioning the status quo, you will create the life you desire.

Are you eager to achieve all this? Do you want to regain control of your life? Do you want to unleash your true potential and create the future you desire? If yes, this is the perfect book for you. So come on, let's get started right away!

Chapter 1:
I Promise Myself—There is Always a Way Out

Feeling as if there is no way out of a situation is probably the most frustrating thing you will ever experience. Such situations occur despite doing everything in your power to do the right thing, listen to what others say you are supposed to do, and do what others might have done in similar situations. Regardless of all this, things don't go as planned. While you are struggling, you see others getting on with their lives and feel hopelessly stuck. No one hopes for such situations. You will learn there is always a way out, provided you look for it.

Discover Your Way Out

Time flies. Perhaps it's been days, weeks, months, or even years and you wonder how you ended up here. You start wondering if there is a way out. It might feel as if you are stuck in a never-ending cycle of similar patterns repeating themselves; closing you in. As mentioned, this might not only be frustrating, but it can also be quite overwhelming to do. The sinking realization that you are stuck can immediately drain any motivation to keep going. If it feels like you are stuck, or there is no way out; here are a few ideas you can use.

Don't Live in a Fantasy

A common reason why most women find themselves in situations where they believe there is no way out is because they are living a fantasy lifestyle. Many believe that the sole purpose in life is to be happy. Self-help gurus and lifestyle experts claim happiness is a spiritual experience that encourages you to live with grace, gratitude, and love every second of the day. This is partially true and instead, becomes the source of our suffering. The world we live in is two-sided. By seeking to live a happy life, we are chasing only one side of it and the other is ignored. When this happens, it becomes quite tiring and overwhelming. Remember, every coin has two sides. You cannot concentrate on one and ignore the other believing it's not a part of the same coin. If you keep doing this, you are living in a fantasy. This is one of the reasons why many believe they are stuck and don't realize until it's too late.

There are ups and downs in life. It's not always peaches and rainbows. There will be obstacles and setbacks you need to overcome. This cannot be overlooked. Every experience in life, whether it is good or bad, is a learning moment. So, stop worrying about things when they don't go your way. Instead, understand it's just a part of life. At times, there will be situations where everything that's happening will seem negative. After a while, you realize it was a life lesson you needed to learn. Let's assume you were at a job that drained you mentally, physically, and emotionally. However, everything you learned in that previous job prepared you for other things in life. So, the seemingly bad experience wasn't all that bad and was just a life lesson.

Similarly, you might be in a terrible situation because someone betrayed you. Instead of feeling bad and becoming miserable thinking you were betrayed, look for those who are still standing by your side. It shows you who means well and who will support you.

Understand Your Vision

If you feel stuck in a situation and think there is no way out, understand what you want to do and determine your vision for the future. Chances are you have no intention of thinking about your vision right now. Regardless of how stressful the situation is, understanding your vision is crucial. Your vision acts as a homing beacon and helps ensure you are on the right track; taking the right steps to attain your goals. It allows you to utilize the existing situations to create a life you desire.

By understanding your vision, it becomes easier to determine everything you can do differently to attain it. This helps, especially when it feels like there is no way out.

It helps you see the bigger picture and understand that the existing circumstances are just a part of life—not the end.

The Period Involved

Whenever you are going through any troubling circumstances, it can feel like the misery is endless. A good thing about life is nothing is constant. The only constant thing is change. So, regardless of how it seems right now, whatever you are dealing with will not be permanent. Everything is temporary. There is no way to determine how long you will need to get out of a given situation. Different factors and variables influence this answer. Fortunately, you have total control over your life and can decide how you want to move on. The steps you take right now will determine whether you are moving away from the situation right away, or will be there for a while longer. Start focusing on your vision, take the right steps, and you will get out of any undesirable situation.

Getting Through Tough Spots

We all tend to go through tough times. This is the reality of life. There will be instances when things just don't go your way regardless of what you do. During such tough times, maintaining a positive mindset is probably the most difficult thing you can do. Good and bad are two sides of the same coin. So, it is important to understand that life will always be good or bad. The best thing you can do is understand how to get through such tough times.

Bad Times Aren't Forever

Change is the only constant in life. While going through a rough spot, it might seem like your troubles are never-ending. It is important to remember that everything ends and therefore, even bad times will end. All that matters is how you view the happenings in your life. Every negative event is often more magnified by our overactive minds than it actually is in reality. Even the worst will pass. Once you understand that bad times will secede, it will lift your spirits and motivation to keep going.

Think About the Past

Were there any situations where you thought, "this is it. This is how things end?" If yes, you aren't alone. We all experience different situations we think we cannot make it through. Yet here we are! You have made it through every situation that seemed dire at one point. If it feels like you have hit a rough spot in life, remind yourself of all the hurdles you have overcome so far. Every instance you thought you would not make it through was a life lesson. They were opportunities for you to grow, develop, and become the person you are today. Use them as a reminder to replenish your self-confidence and motivation to keep going.

You Are Stronger Than You Believe

When you are facing hardships, it becomes easier to indulge in negative self-talk. This essentially means you start focusing more on your flaws instead of strengths. This kind of thinking can make you feel like you are incapable of overcoming difficult circumstances in life. Well, all the negative thoughts in your head are worse than the situation itself. Remember, all your worries are just thoughts and there is no reason why you need to accept them as the truth. As with anyone else out there, you have your strengths and weaknesses. While dealing with difficulties, it's important to remind yourself of your strengths instead of focusing only on weaknesses. Once you do this, you will realize you are stronger than you believe. By shifting your perception toward yourself for the better, dealing with challenges and obstacles becomes easier.

Everything Is a Learning Experience

When you are facing difficulties, you might start questioning why these things keep happening to you. In such situations, a better perspective is to start viewing all the hardships as a learning opportunity. Ask yourself,

"What is life trying to teach me right now?" When you treat obstacles as a learning opportunity, it becomes easier to work on yourself and avoid making the same mistakes in the future. Life is a process of trial and error. There will be things that go your way and others that don't. Whatever happens, is happening for a reason. Don't see failure as an indicator that you are not headed in the right direction. Instead, think of it as a learning experience that is pushing you toward your goals.

Everyone Faces Trouble

The world we live in is dominated by social media. Whenever you open any of your social media profiles, chances are you will be flooded with images of others living seemingly perfect lives. This can increase unnecessary comparison that ultimately makes you feel bad about yourself. Do yourself a favor and stop indulging in such unhealthy comparisons. Remember, success and failure are two sides of the same coin. Life isn't just about happiness and it is riddled with difficulties too. To truly enjoy happiness, you need to overcome difficulties. No one is free from problems. You are extremely aware of everything going wrong in your life because it's happening to you. This doesn't mean others don't have any problems. When you feel alone or feel as though the universe is plotting against you, remember that everyone has their share of troubles. You will not know what true happiness or success means if you don't stumble and fall.

Ask For Help When Needed

You are not alone. If you are facing difficulties, no one is stopping you from asking for help. Asking for help when needed is a sign of self-confidence and self-respect. It shows you what you can and cannot do. It takes a lot of self-confidence to ask someone else for help. Whether it's emotional or mental support, depending on others will make your burdens seem less overwhelming. Knowing that you can count on others will improve your self-confidence—to deal with the challenges that come your way.

Practice Gratitude

Start practicing gratitude so it becomes easier to make it through tough times. Even when everything else seems to be going wrong in life, there will be things you are grateful for. Whether it's a loving partner, family, or a job you enjoy, these are all blessings. Start counting your blessings instead of worrying about everything that's missing in your life. By cultivating an attitude of gratitude, dealing with tough circumstances becomes easier. Even your troubles will seem more bearable and less challenging.

Stop Feeling Stuck

There will always be instances when you feel stuck for one reason or another. Whether it's a relationship, career, or just life, you will invariably feel stuck. When you feel stuck, you cannot feel good about anything. You tend to lose track of yourself and the choices you make, and start concentrating on all the wrong things. If you want to get through tough spots, and move on in life, work on shifting your perspective. If this happens, remember the following.

When you feel stuck, it's a sign that you need to make some changes. Whether it's changing your outlook toward life, habits, or working on something new, change is the answer to stop feeling stuck. Usually, we tend to feel stuck when things aren't working for us anymore. Whether it's a relationship, job, or anything else, it's a sign that you need to concentrate on something else. Making a change is not easy and it can also be painful. But it is necessary to grow. If you feel stuck, it means you must start focusing on your personal growth.

When you are feeling stuck it can be quite overwhelming. Many believe the only way to stop feeling stuck is by doing something significant. Well, this isn't always possible. You don't have to do anything substantial immediately. Instead, concentrate on taking small steps. Even changing yourself by 1% daily results in a cumulative 37% change within a year. By concentrating on small things, it becomes easier to take action.

If you don't take any action and keep waiting for things to change, you are in for a nasty shock. Nothing will change unless you want it to change. If you keep waiting for your life to change or for something to happen, you cannot get ahead. Remember, you own the power to change your life. Unless you want to, you cannot make anything happen.

When you are feeling stuck, it might feel like you don't know what to do. It's okay if you don't have everything figured out. Even those who are extremely successful don't have everything figured out. This is perfectly normal and you should expect it. When you are feeling calmer you might experience a sense of emptiness and numbness. Remember, all these feelings are temporary and therefore, they should not prevent you from changing. It is okay if you cannot see the result right now. Instead, concentrate on just taking the steps required to get moving. Once you take the first step, it builds the momentum to keep going.

When you are feeling stuck, negativity takes center stage. You cannot see anything good in your life if you're surrounded by negativity. The best way to make room for good is by letting go of all the undesirable and toxic things. This means you need to start eliminating toxicity from your life. Regardless of whether it's a relationship or a habit, eliminate it if it is toxic. Once you let go of all this negativity, you are automatically freeing up space for better things. If anything or anyone isn't adding value to your life and is instead bringing you down, you don't need them.

At times, even a new beginning can seem like an ending. The problem with endings is they aren't always happy. Even if your ending isn't picture-perfect, you now have an opportunity to start something better. If you are going through tough times in life, remember they are only temporary and will soon come to an end. When you are feeling stuck, it becomes difficult to see any available opportunities even if they are staring you in the face. The only way to capitalize on these opportunities is by letting go of certain things. Even if an ending makes you sad and disappointed, it should not prevent you from seeing the new beginning on the horizon. If something has come to an end, close the chapter and move on.

If you are feeling stuck, take some time for self-introspection. Analyze if you are living for yourself or are living someone else's life for them. Are you doing things because you like them or are you doing them because others tell you to? If you have been living your life according to someone else's guidelines, stop it right now. Instead, start doing things you want to do. After all, this life is yours and yours alone. You have the power to do what you want. You can ask for suggestions and opinions before making a decision; as long as the decision is yours, it's all good. If others are deciding for you, it's time to take back your sense of control. Start concentrating on discovering things you enjoy. It's not bad to spend time with yourself. Invest in improving your self-awareness. Question your beliefs before accepting them as the ultimate truth. At times, you also need to take a step back to see the bigger picture. Apart from that, start establishing and implementing boundaries. Do things that feel right and good to you. Stop letting the fear of failure prevent you from doing anything.

If something is meant to be, it will happen. At times, regardless of how hard you try, some things don't pan out. Instead of feeling discouraged in such instances, it's better to take a break. Let things be however they are right now. If you cannot fix something, move on to a different avenue. When the time is right and you are ready for it, the things you desire will happen. If you keep doing the same thing expecting different results, it's insanity! So, stop trying and concentrate on changing instead.

A simple way to stop feeling stuck is by letting things be. Give yourself a break and stop overthinking. Whatever happens, happens for a reason. You cannot control everything. Once you make your peace with it, concentrating on a solution becomes easier. If you are facing a problem, what good will it do if you keep focusing solely on the problem? You cannot change the situation unless you find a solution. The only way forward is to focus on the solution. This simple change in mindset makes it easier to stop feeling stuck.

Learn to let go of the past. You cannot move forward if you are constantly looking back. The past cannot be undone. Regardless of how hard you try and hope for it, there is not much you can do to alter what happened. Instead, look to the future. Every moment you have right now is an opportunity to create the future you desire. The best is yet to come and you have the power to make it happen.

Chapter 2:
You Can Dream Big and
Achieve the Extraordinary

We all have dreams and aspirations. So why are only a few successful? Why are only a few people extraordinary? It's because they are not scared of dreaming big and did not shy away from working hard to achieve the extraordinary. We all have immense potential within. Unfortunately, people and circumstances prevent us from dreaming big and achieving the extraordinary. The gender stereotype cannot be ignored, especially in today's world. Most girls have grown up listening to what they should do and how they should be. Societal conditioning and our experiences have taught us what we are supposed to do. Most of us are reconciling with our own expectations and dreams because we are told women need to be a certain way instead of living the lives we desire.

Remember, you are the only person standing between your dreams and aspirations and the success you desire. You have more potential within you than you ever thought. You can channel your dormant and ignored potential to become extraordinary. Why settle for ordinary when you are so much more than that?

Don't Let Circumstances and People Control You

How you live your life is entirely in your hands. No one can take this power away from you unless you consciously give it away. Remember, you are in the driver's seat and therefore, are in charge of coursing through life on your own terms. If you are letting others control you and situations influence you, you are not living on your own terms. To determine whether others are influencing you or not, you need to ask yourself these questions.

- Are people and circumstances regulating your mood, state of mind, and life in general?

- How do you feel when others criticize you?

- Imagine you are driving and another driver is driving quite recklessly in front of you. Do you feel frustrated or annoyed because of it?

If yes, you are not alone. We all tend to feel like this at one point. This is a part of life. The problem starts when you spend all your conscious time and energy thinking about such incidents instead of concentrating on life. If you start taking everything that happens quite personally, you become inefficient in general. It doesn't matter whether it's your personal or professional life, if you let circumstances and people control you, you are not truly living. In a way, you are letting them control whatever happens in your life.

Regardless of how hard you try, you cannot regulate people, circumstances, and situations. This is how life works and you need to make your peace with it. You cannot control what others say or do. However, you have complete control over how you respond to different situations. Life is not about what happens to you. Instead, it is about how you deal with whatever happens. You can teach yourself to respond differently, both emotionally and mentally. If you are letting others bother you and regulate your life, it is your decision. This is a choice you have made unknowingly.

Think about the following questions for a moment.

- Are you dwelling on incidents that hurt you?

- Are your negative reactions to situations hurting you further?

- Are you taking things—especially criticism, quite personally?

- Do you feel like a puppet whose strings are being pulled by others?

If yes, you are letting people and situations dictate your life.

If you are experiencing any of the above-mentioned scenarios, here is a simple exercise you can use to loosen the hold others and circumstances have on you. Think of it as first aid; especially when your emotions are running high and you don't feel in control of yourself. The first thing you need to do is stop whatever you are doing. Take a break, close your eyes, and breathe in and out. Start focusing on how you inhale and exhale. Before you decide to say or do anything, breathe deeply a couple of times. Any negative thought you are thinking right now should be replaced with a positive one. If you are not able to do this, try pushing the negative thought away. Concentrate on relaxing your body. Physical relaxation promotes mental relaxation. Once you are calmer, you can think clearly.

When you do this, you are essentially detaching yourself from the scenario emotionally. By regaining control of your emotions, you can clearly think about what you want to say and do. This ensures you are not saying or doing anything you might regret later. By acting and responding calmly and with logic, devoid of any emotional agitation, making better decisions becomes easier.

You Are in Charge of Your Thoughts

If you want to stop others from governing your life, you need to come to the simple realization that you are in charge here. If you have allowed someone else to sit in the driver's seat, it's time to regain control of your life. The first step toward doing this is to understand your thoughts. Your thoughts are your own. Perhaps the hardest battle in your life will be with yourself. Avoid overthinking and instead, concentrate on living the life you want. Prepare yourself to deal with anything that comes your way regardless of whether it is good or bad. Once you accept that you are the only one in charge here, no one can take control away from you.

Stop Expecting

If you don't want others to regulate you, let go of any expectations. Expectations can be quite confining and restrictive. When left unregulated, they can also take a toll on your well-being. If you are doing things because others expect you to, you are not living for yourself. If you are doing things because you are expecting others to reciprocate, you are once again wasting your resources. You will be in for plenty of pleasant surprises once you stop expecting. This also reduces negative reactions. Stop focusing on every thought that includes the words should and must. When you do this, you automatically shift toward a positive perspective.

Become Goal-Orientated

Goals give you a sense of purpose. When you have something to look forward to, regulating your emotions becomes easier. It also encourages you to start taking daily action needed for a specific goal. If it feels like something else is regulating your life, ask yourself whether a specific thought or action will bring you closer to your goal. If it doesn't, then you don't need to waste any time dwelling on it. By establishing meaningful goals, you are automatically adding more value and meaning to your life.

Understand Yourself

You have won half the battle once you start understanding yourself. Take time for self-introspection and concentrate on your true self which lies within. If you take a moment and think about everything, you will realize where your priorities lie. There might be areas you have overlooked because until now, your life was regulated by others and certain situations. When you start becoming mindful of yourself and develop self-awareness, you start appreciating everything in your life. This also reduces the victim mindset. If you keep victimizing yourself, it will make you miserable. It will also make you feel stuck and shackled. You aren't a victim and therefore, there is no reason to start behaving like one.

A Pinch of Salt

We all are different and wired differently. This means we experience life and situations quite differently. This also means we will have varying opinions. Accept your uniqueness and learn to take things with a pinch of salt. This also ensures you stop taking things personally. For instance, dealing with criticism, especially when it comes from someone you love, is quite tough. Regardless of whether it is positive or negative criticism, it still hurts. The problem here is not the criticism. Instead, it's how you are absorbing it. Once you start taking things with a pinch of salt, you can see the bigger picture. It also helps to understand that just because someone else says something it doesn't make it true. It's simply an opinion. Whether you accept it or not is your choice. If you don't agree with what's said, you don't have to accept it.

Avoid Pity Parties

Indulging in self-pity will make you feel more miserable than you already do. It also takes away your sense of control. By pitying yourself, you have essentially made yourself a victim of circumstances in life. This is not okay. Instead of pushing away your emotions, learn to deal with them. Don't engage in self-pity because it does not get you anything. Instead, you'll start feeling more stuck than ever. Whenever you start pitying yourself, replace it with gratitude. Concentrate on all the good you have and the desire to indulge in self-pity goes away.

You Have The Power

If you don't want circumstances and people regulating your life, it's important to understand you are wholly and solely responsible for your thoughts and decisions. Whatever you feel and experience is the result of your cognitive processes. Once you learn to gain control over this, you will realize you are no longer living a life regulated by others. Whenever you experience an unsettling thought or emotion, acknowledge and accept it. Anything you experience is yours. Instead of blaming others or situations for your emotions, simply accept them. Blame breeds more contempt. So, stop looking for different reasons to blame; instead, accept your thoughts, feelings, and experiences as they are.

Learn to Dream Big

If you want to achieve the extraordinary, you need to learn to dream big. Whether it's gender bias or societal conditioning, women are constantly controlled by different external circumstances and factors. If you keep living your life regulated by others, you're not living. Don't be scared to dream big.

Don't Be Scared

Dreams are not restricted to the time when you are sleeping. Several women don't realize what they are truly capable of because they're scared of dreaming big. Nothing is impossible; provided you are willing to make the required effort to achieve it. Hard work, determination, planning, and consistency are the key ingredients essential for attaining success. You are always capable of more than you believe. This is one of the reasons why you shouldn't be afraid to dream big. Remember, this is just a dream and unless you work toward it, it will not become a reality.

Start Planning

A problem with dreaming big is that most people get overwhelmed when they look at their dream. Well, don't be scared because everything is doable. Instead of believing your dreams are overwhelming, take a step back and see what you can do to accomplish them. You don't have to accomplish everything right away. Life is a journey and working toward your big dreams is a journey too. Whenever you have a dream, break it down into smaller and doable steps. If you want to run a marathon, you need to run regularly and cover long distances. The first step is to prepare yourself mentally and physically to run the marathon. To do this, you need to work on improving your strength, endurance, and stamina daily. This is a small step and you have complete control to accomplish this. So, start planning how you want to achieve your goal by breaking it down into smaller steps.

Tracking Your Progress

Whenever you are working toward a goal or a dream, ensure that you are tracking the progress you make. Instead of getting overwhelmed by looking at the distance you need to cover, congratulate yourself on the distance you have covered. Every milestone or small step you achieve along the way brings you a step closer to your dream. Even if you're not where you want to be right now, you can still get there.

Stay Motivated

Don't underestimate the importance of motivation if you are working toward a big goal. Motivation might not always come easily or stay for long. However, with a little practice, you can keep yourself motivated every day. As mentioned, start concentrating on the small steps you take daily and the progress you are making. This is one of the simplest ways to stay motivated. Apart from that, focus on the reasons to achieve your goals and your motivation will be renewed.

Support System

You are never alone. All you need to do is ask for support and you will be given what you need. There will be days when it feels like there's no one with you and you're all alone on this journey. Well, all of this is in your head. You can create a support system for yourself. Your family members, friends, loved ones, acquaintances, and pretty much anyone you want can be a part of your support system. On days when the going gets tough, your support system will give you the courage and motivation required to keep going. You can also find a coach or mentor to act as your support system.

Start Taking Action

We all want to accomplish different things in life. Unless we take action, we cannot get anything done. Regardless of how well laid out your plans are, they account for nothing without action. Don't get scared and overwhelmed looking at the journey ahead of you. instead, take the first step. By taking the first step, you are building the required momentum to keep going. Concentrate on taking small steps daily and you will reach your destination within no time.

Embracing Failure

Don't shy away from failure. Prepare yourself for obstacles, setbacks, and challenges on this journey you are going on. Hurdles are a part of life. You cannot achieve success without facing failure. Don't be scared of failing; it is a learning curve. Start embracing failure because it's an inevitable part of life. All those who are successful failed multiple times before achieving success. Failure teaches you more about yourself than success will. While dealing with failure, the only thing that matters is your attitude. If you believe failure is the end of the road, it will be the end.

On the other hand, if you view it as a learning opportunity, dealing with failure becomes easy. Whenever you are dreaming, believe in yourself. Unless you believe in your dream and yourself, you cannot succeed.

Don't Stop Believing

It doesn't matter whether your dreams make sense to others. It doesn't matter whether they believe in you or not. When you believe in yourself, nothing is impossible. If you are prepared to dedicate the time and effort to achieving your goals, you can get there. Push yourself even when the going gets tough. Maintaining a positive attitude, especially on this journey toward attaining big goals is important.

Chapter 3:
Truth Hurts—Nothing Is
Impossible: I Am Possible!

You can be anything you put your mind to! You might have come across a similar phrase at one point or another in your life. Ask yourself whether you are living life on your own terms. If you aren't, then is there something preventing you from living the life you desire? Does it feel like gender stereotypes and societal expectations are preventing you from living to the fullest? Are you shackled by these expectations that are preventing you from soaring? Well, it is time to break free of all these constraints because nothing is impossible. If you believe you can, you can!

Things to Remember

Have you ever read or heard a fairytale? A typical fairytale features a damsel in distress who needs to be rescued by a knight in shining armor. All the fairy tales we love and grew up listening to feature a similar storyline. When the entire society we live in has been conditioned to believe women need to behave and live a certain way, breaking free of such a restrictive mold is not easy. Women are expected to bear children, settle early in life, and essentially play the role of nurturer. Any woman who wants to do something that doesn't fit this predefined mold is viewed with contempt. She is called difficult, labeled mean names, and her dreams are labeled as impossible. Well, we are all human and are created equally. It is our time to rise up and shine. If you are trying to achieve the impossible, remind yourself that nothing is ever truly impossible. It's just that certain things take longer than others. Here are certain things you need to remember while chasing the impossible.

Negative Beliefs Are Possible

Understand that all negative beliefs are incredibly powerful. Once you start believing something is absolutely impossible, it can turn into a self-fulfilling prophecy. When you believe you cannot do something, this thought slowly chips away at your self-confidence and motivation to even try. If both these factors go away, the chances of attaining the goal itself become impossible. For instance, if you believe you cannot achieve anything worthwhile because no one will pay attention to you due to your gender, the chances of even trying something different will reduce. If you start accepting this belief as the absolute truth, what is the point of even trying when you will not achieve success?

Positive Beliefs Triumph Over Negative Ones

If negative beliefs are powerful, positive ones are even more powerful. When you find a dream or a vision to focus on, put your mind to it and work to attain it, your chances of success automatically increase. For instance, Mahatma Gandhi wouldn't have led India toward independence if he believed it would be impossible to relinquish the hold of the British on India. Similarly, Martin Luther King Jr., might not have managed to achieve civil rights in the United States if he believed this goal was impossible. When you start believing you can and are capable of doing what you put your mind to, finding a way to make it happen becomes easier.

Authority Isn't Synonymous with Knowing

Most of us believe authority is synonymous with knowledge. Our confidence in our abilities diminishes when someone in a position of authority tells us we cannot or are not capable of doing something. Whether it's a teacher or parent, this kind of negativity from someone in an authoritative position can be damaging to our self-confidence. When you start believing someone else's opinion of you, you fail to see all the good within. If you want to accomplish anything in life, it's important to understand yourself. Learn to become aware of your strengths and weaknesses. Once you have this awareness, nothing else can stop you. For instance, if you were constantly told by your teachers at school that you are not good at science or math, chances are you have lived your entire life believing this. You stop trying to change when someone already has a poor opinion of you because you are living up to other's ideas and expectations of what you should or shouldn't do.

Understand What is Possible

Instead of worrying about the impossible, start believing that everything is possible. You need to create a fearless state of mind. Whether it's the fear of failure or a worry that you don't have the required skills, it's time to put them to rest. These fears can be paralyzing when left unchecked. Fears also prevent you from seeing and understanding the reality of things. They take your focus away from the bigger picture and instead, make you concentrate on all things trivial. Always remember that your fears are a hundred times worse in your head than they actually are.

Instead of believing your fears, take a moment to think about your life in general. Was there something you managed to achieve that you thought was impossible? Whether it is surviving a breakup or standing up to your parents, chances are some aspects in your professional or personal life would have been impossible in the past. Well, here you are today. What does this tell you? Nothing is impossible once you decide to go for it. If you have accomplished anything you ever thought was impossible, make a note of it. Always carry this note with you for added motivation. So, whenever you start doubting yourself, remind yourself of the distance you have already covered. This will ensure the embers of motivation within you don't die.

Overcome the Impossible

Our society has come a long way toward establishing gender equality, but we have a long way to go before we fully achieve it. For now, it's nothing but a dream. This is one of the reasons why it seems women have to work harder than their male counterparts to achieve the same success. From societal expectations to familiar commitments, different factors tend to become hurdles that all women need to face at one point or another.

The idea of the impossible is subjective and changes from one person to another. A girl from a conservative household might struggle to convince her parents to let her study abroad. For her, this is an impossible task. Similarly, a new mother might want to become an entrepreneur and is told her dream is impossible. We all have different ideas, goals, and targets that are labeled impossible for one reason or another. Even if they are not labeled so, we believe they are impossible. Regardless of all this, you have the power to make them possible. To do this, you need conviction, resilience, dedication, and hard work. When you commit yourself to it, you can achieve whatever you put your mind to. That said, overcoming seemingly impossible situations isn't always easy, but is doable.

Don't Get Stuck on Specifics

To overcome the impossible, you need to establish certain goals and start working toward them religiously. That said, you should also leave some room for flexibility. The future you desire to create shouldn't be set in stone. Ensure the idea you are working on and the future you want to create can evolve simultaneously. Don't get so caught up with your vision that you cannot let it go. In such circumstances, your commitment and dedication will soon turn into arrogance. If you become arrogant about the future you want to create, it is similar to getting into a staring contest with a tsunami. There is no possible way in which you will come out the winner. Avoid letting your commitment turn to arrogance and instead, let serendipity do its work. Be willing to let your idea change. With time and experience, your priorities will change and with it, the future you want to create will also change. Do not establish a fort wall of defenses around your idea by getting stuck on the specifics. Instead, let it flow freely so you have the room required to create the future you desire.

Don't Overlook Naysayers

Whenever you are trying to overcome the impossible, the naysayers will say you cannot possibly make it happen. We all have different perspectives toward life which results in different opinions, ideas, and notions. There is no reason why everyone would think like you do and believe your ideas are good. All that matters is whether the idea makes sense to you. Whenever you are dealing with naysayers, instead of brushing away what they're saying, use it to improve yourself. If they are raising any objections, use them to build value. If someone says you cannot do something, they are saying so because of a specific reason. Use that reason as a challenge to overcome it. In this way, all the naysayers are doing is presenting potential problems, challenges, and setbacks you might face on your journey. Use these instances to prepare yourself for them and look for ways to avoid such potential problems.

Overestimate Available Resources

Whenever you are chasing something that seems impossible, you should always overestimate the resources available. Whether you want to change your job or move to a new city, you need resources to do it. Overestimate the resources you will need to make such a change. When you overestimate, you are essentially pushing yourself to do better. When you underestimate the resources required to support the change, chances of disappointment increase. When you expect to fall short, you are ready for it and have some resources in reserve as well. Creating this additional buffer will give you the needed flexibility to change the impossible.

Let Go of Your Constraints

Whenever you are chasing after a dream or a goal, you need to break free of any self-imposed constraints. It's not just others whom you need to ignore; you should also learn to ignore certain constraints you have created for yourself. Believing that you don't have the required self-confidence or motivation to go ahead with a plan is a self-constraint. Similarly, believing that you will not succeed is a self-constraint. All these negative thoughts and beliefs are preventing you from doing your best. It will not always be easy to go where you want to. That said, you're the only one preventing yourself from going there. Stop sabotaging your vision and instead, concentrate on the steps you can take to achieve it.

Achieve the Impossible with a Positive Mindset

All the different beliefs that regulate how you make sense of yourself, the world, and life in general, are known as your mindset. Your mindset matters because it determines how you feel, think, and behave at any given point. The age-old question of "is the glass half-empty or half-full?" shows your mindset. If you believe the glass is half empty, it shows pessimism while the latter shows optimism. Maintaining a positive mindset doesn't mean you don't have to face or overcome any challenges in life. Instead, it is about believing in your abilities and knowing you can overcome any challenge that comes your way. If you want to achieve the impossible, your mindset matters a lot.

A negative mindset prompts you to see all the difficulties or problems in any situation. On the other hand, a positive mindset encourages you to believe in yourself. To cultivate a positive mindset, here are some tips you can use.

Choose an Impossible Mission

The first step of maintaining a positive mindset, especially while trying to achieve the impossible is to select your mission. What is the specific thing you are trying to attain? Whether it's your personal or professional life, you need to have a goal in mind. Without this, you cannot make the most of the resources available. Remember, the resources available will always be fixed while their uses will be unlimited. The dream or goal you want to concentrate on should be something you believe in. You need to be enthusiastic and determined to achieve said goal. You should also be willing to make the required effort toward working on it. So, what is your mission impossible? What do you want to achieve that feels impossible right now? Just because something seems out of reach doesn't mean it will always stay that way. With time, effort, dedication, motivation, and resilience, you can improve and grow.

Stop Focusing on Perfection

If you want to move ahead in life, you need to stop concentrating on perfection. Perfection is the enemy of action. We all make mistakes and there is no way around it. When you concentrate on being perfect, it reduces your motivation to keep going, especially when you make a mistake. Perfection also stops you from taking action. Instead, you will start waiting until the conditions are perfect or the time is right before taking any action. If you think and function like this, you will never get things done. Instead of perfection, concentrate on the efforts you make. There is more to life than just attaining results. Do not be discouraged by any setbacks and start learning from your mistakes. When you do this, you grow and develop.

Don't Look Back

If you want to achieve the impossible, you need to concentrate on taking one step at a time. Any goal you want to achieve is a combination of small steps taken over a period of time. How can you move forward if you keep looking back? Whatever happened in the past should stay there. It means you should stop holding on to the past. Keep yourself open to all opportunities and experiences in life. When you do this, you keep moving ahead. This brings you closer to achieving the impossible.

Be Flexible

You need to establish your goals so there is room for flexibility. Keep taking action daily and evaluate all the progress you make. Regardless of how perfect a plan seems, you need to tweak and adjust your approach to reach the destination you want. This essentially means, you should not just have one plan, but multiple plans to achieve the goal you have in mind. When there is room for flexibility, taking action becomes easier.

Be Loyal to Progress

Rome was not built in a day. To achieve incredible results, you need to make progress. Concentrate on taking small steps daily. Any goal you establish should be broken down into smaller goals. Prioritize the different activities and tasks that need to be performed while committing yourself to your goal. Plan things in such a manner that you don't leave any stone unturned. Think of different ways you can concentrate on your goal and work toward the progress you desire. When you concentrate on the progress instead of the results, achieving your goals becomes easier. All the progress you make also acts as the motivation required to keep going.

Brainstorming

If you want to achieve the impossible, you need to keep an open mind. This means you should be willing to brainstorm different ideas. Don't just keep your goals to yourself. Start sharing your dreams and aspirations with your close circle; those you trust and love unconditionally. No two individuals are alike and therefore, our perspectives and approach toward life differ. When you keep an open mind, it becomes easier to see the same situation from multiple perspectives. The ability to do this improves your creativity and makes it easier to grab any new ideas that come your way.

Motivate Yourself

You need to stay motivated to get ahead in life. This motivation should come from within. Whenever you are establishing a goal, ensure that it motivates you. Without motivation, even a small obstacle seems overwhelming and extremely challenging. When you are motivated, your commitment to the goal automatically improves. There will be days when everything goes your way and others when it seems like nothing is working. On such days, your motivation is all that keeps you going. So, before you establish a goal, ensure that it is something you want to achieve. Make sure you are working on the goal because you want to achieve it and not because of someone else's reasons. Use your personal reasons as motivation to achieve the impossible.

Action-Oriented Mindset

While we're talking about maintaining a positive mindset, you must develop an action-oriented mindset. It's not just about setting big goals for yourself or dreaming big. If you are passive, you are not making the most of opportunities. Instead, you are simply letting life happen and pass you by. Unless you take action, you cannot get the results you desire. If you keep postponing and procrastinating, you will never achieve your goals. To become successful, you need to understand there's plenty of action involved in it. Learning to take the right action at the right time will propel you toward success. Become proactive and create a mindset that enables you to take action.

Whenever you take positive action or a step that brings you closer to your goal, it automatically increases your self-confidence. When you start feeling confident about your abilities it increases self-reliance. A combination of these factors will improve your self-esteem and motivation. If you want to develop an action-oriented mindset, here are some simple steps you should remember.

The first step is to anticipate all obstacles or challenges you might face. Whenever you are planning, ensure that you have one or two backup plans in mind. Regardless of how well laid out your plans are, life is unpredictable. Don't, even for a second, believe that circumstances will stay constant. It's not just the circumstances; chances are your goals and dreams also change as you grow and experience new things. So, whenever you are planning, ensure that you have a couple of backups in mind. The backup plan should also have an exit strategy. Knowing when to cut your losses and exit is as important as having a plan of action to get started on working toward the goal. Yes, life is indeed unpredictable. That said, you can take certain steps to reduce the risk you are exposed to. Equipping yourself to deal with different challenges and obstacles you might face is better than not having a backup plan. By reducing your risk of exposure, your chances of success increase.

Remember that life is full of opportunities. All that matters is how you view them. For instance, even a failure or setback you experience is an opportunity to learn and grow. If you view failure as the end of the journey, it will become a self-fulfilling prophecy. Instead, think of different circumstances as opportunities presented by life for your growth and development. To improve your confidence and overcome any fears you might face, take action. It's okay to try things and it is perfectly normal to fail. Don't shy away from failure and instead prepare yourself to move on. Preparation is the key to success. Any action you take is better than not doing anything. You will learn a lot even when you don't succeed.

Whenever any challenge crops up, do not shy away from it. Instead, face it head-on. This is the only way to move forward. You cannot become unstoppable or achieve the impossible if you give up whenever you are facing a challenge or an obstacle. Start believing that you have all the required skills and abilities to deal with the challenges. When your self-confidence improves, your ability to deal with circumstances also improves. This becomes easier, especially when you have a backup in place.

Whenever you are facing a challenge, it's quite easy to start overthinking all the different solutions available. If you want to get ahead, you need to stop thinking and start moving. It essentially means stop contemplating too much about the merits or demerits of a specific solution or an option. Instead, implement a plan and see if there is any room for improvement. There is no reason to believe a plan cannot be improved or changed. Unless you try, you will never know. By creating a mindset of action, you are motivated to take action and stop thinking.

If you have made up your mind to do something, implement it immediately. Do not tell yourself you will get to it later. later will never come. When you put things on hold, procrastination creeps in. If anything can be done today, get on it immediately. There is time for other things later. While deciding what to act on, concentrate on the long-term benefits associated with a specific step. Don't just concentrate on immediate rewards; look for long-term value and benefits.

Daily Habits for Positivity

If you want to maintain a positive attitude, understand that it is a continuous process—an ongoing journey, and not a 100 meter dash. By consciously teaching yourself to build and maintain a positive attitude, improving the overall quality of your life becomes easier. Use these practical suggestions to develop daily habits that will help develop and maintain a positive attitude.

Regardless of everything that happens, one thing you can control is how you react to the external world. You are the only one capable of determining your reality. Whenever anything happens, you have the power to decide how you want to react. For instance, if you were turned down for a promotion at work, you can either engage in self-criticism and feel hopeless, or treat it as an opportunity to improve your existing skill set. By understanding that you determine your reality, it will automatically make you feel more in control of your life.

What is the first thing you do as soon as you open your eyes in the morning? Do you check your phone, email, or browse through social media? Well, instead of wasting precious morning hours like this, utilize them to do something more productive. When you start your day on a good note, It sets a positive tone for the rest of the day. Ensure that you take some time for self-reflection, planning, and setting daily goals in the morning. Apart from this, take some time for exercising or meditating, and eating a healthy breakfast. Feeding your body is as important as feeding your mind and soul.

Exercising regularly is an important part of improving your overall well-being. Exercising not only benefits your physical health but improves your mental and emotional health too. It is a great stress reliever as well. Start your day by exercising for around 20-30 minutes. You might believe you'll feel too tired for the rest of the day. Well, exercise gets your metabolism revving. It also increases the production of endorphins, also known as feel-good hormones. This little extra boost that your metabolism and mind get makes it easier to maintain a positive attitude.

Apart from taking care of your body, you must pay attention to your mental and emotional well-being too. A simple way to add a dash of positivity to your daily routine is by reading inspiring books, listening to podcasts, or watching videos. You can get inspired by the lives of others as well. You can also use their experiences to improve your life and yourself. Feed your mind inspirational and motivational content in the morning to maintain a positive mindset.

Every day, take some time and make a note of any negative self-thoughts you had during the day. When you write it all down, you can see and analyze whether these thoughts are facts or not. It also gives you a chance to refute and replace a specific thought if it doesn't serve any purpose, this simple activity helps slowly condition and change your thought process for the better.

If you want to maintain a positive mindset, give yourself a break. Take the time needed to rest and recharge your batteries. Unwind and destress after a tiring day. Whether it is spending time with your friends or taking your pet for a walk, do something that helps you relax. Giving your brain positive fodder to ponder upon is as important as giving it a break.

You don't have to start implementing all these suggestions at once. Instead, take things one day at a time. Concentrate on making one change and then another. A gradual approach will make it easier to attain significant results.

Chapter 4:
The Empowerment of Failure— Metamorphosis—Making Strides Toward Positive Change

Your thoughts are incredibly powerful because they affect your mood and emotions. Since your mood and emotions are responsible for your behavior and all the actions you take in life, regulating your thoughts is important. You might not have paid any attention to it, but there's a constant internal dialogue going on in your head. If you stay quiet for a minute, you can hear this internal conversation. This is known as self-talk.

Self-talk is natural and we do this for long as we are awake. Unfortunately, most of us aren't conscious of this self-talk. The more aware you become of this, the easier it is to influence your mind to take positive action. If you are constantly critiquing yourself or focusing solely on your shortcomings, your self-talk is negative. If you have such a poor opinion of yourself, how can you ever get anything done? A simple example of negative self-talk is telling yourself, "I am not smart enough to do this." When you are facing challenges, the urge to indulge in negative self-talk increases. This is a subconscious act of self-sabotage.

Practicing Positive Self-Talk

How you talk to yourself determines how you view yourself and your attitude toward life. So, it is always better to concentrate on maintaining a positive internal dialogue to improve your attitude. In this section, let's look at simple suggestions you can use to start practicing positive self-talk.

No Negativity

We all experience days when we feel blue. Start paying attention to the company you keep. You will notice you feel different around different people. There will be some who seem to be down all the time. If you are constantly surrounded by such negativity, all traces of positive self-talk will go away. The attitude of others affects your own. Those with a negative attitude will bring you down. Whether it's your coworkers or family members, you don't need any negativity. Try limiting your exposure to such negativity to feel better about yourself.

Become Grateful

A simple way to practice positive self-talk is by concentrating on all the good in your life. It's repeatedly mentioned that gratitude is important for moving ahead. There are plenty of things in life you need to be grateful for. Instead of concentrating on everything that's absent, concentrate on the good. By focusing on the good, you are creating more room for better things in your life. Every day, start spending around 5-10 minutes making a note of all the things you are grateful for.

Stop Comparing

The chances of engaging in negative self-talk increase when you are constantly comparing yourself to others. Remember that no two individuals are alike and therefore, whatever we are experiencing in life will always be different. If you want to feel better about yourself, stop engaging in unnecessary comparisons. Comparison not only breeds contempt, but removes traces of gratitude from your life too. Apart from that, it can also make you feel inadequate.

Positive Dialogue

Start paying extra attention to the words you use while talking to others. You might not have given it any conscious thought, but how you speak to others also dictates the words you use while engaging in self-talk. Negative self-talk increases when your mind is dominated by negative thoughts. How do you talk to others in general? For instance, what is the first thing you say as soon as you reach work in the morning? Do you start complaining about little annoyances of the day or concentrate on making the most of the time available? If it's the former, it is time to shift your attitude for the better. Regardless of everything that happens in life, you have complete control over what you think, say, and do. Whether you think negative or positive thoughts, it is entirely up to you. If you say something negative, remember it's a conscious choice you made.

Why is it important to maintain a positive dialogue? If you are thinking negative thoughts, the chances of speaking negatively to others increases. If you are constantly complaining about how your spouse does not clean up after working in the kitchen, you will end up saying this to your spouse too. The only problem is how you present your thoughts might not be ideal and can be negative or seem nagging. Instead, concentrate on using positive and uplifting words to create a better environment in your life. The simplest way to do this is by paying attention to how you talk. Even if you're bothered or worried about something, expressing what you feel and taking your time to talk about what you're experiencing is better than engaging in negative dialogue.

Don't Be Scared of Failure

The fear of failure is quite real and paralyzing to a certain extent. Remember, the road to success is not easy and it is scattered with this fear. All those who are successful in life have encountered failure. The only difference between them and others is they didn't give up. This fear can prevent you from even trying your hand at success. If you let this fear prevent you from doing something, you cannot get anything done.

You Can Succeed

If you want to succeed, you need to start believing in your abilities or skills to succeed. If you don't have this belief, you cannot move ahead in life. If you are constantly second-guessing and doubting everything you say and do, how can you succeed? Remember, you might not succeed on the first attempt. Even if you have to try more than once, you will get there. All that matters is whether you reach the destination or not. instead of the journey ahead of you, think about the distance covered so far. You cannot succeed if you constantly compare yourself to others. Tell yourself you have what it takes to do better in life and move on. Tell yourself you are capable of getting the job done one way or another and getting the job done will become easier.

Use Positive Affirmations

A simple way to put a positive spin on your self-talk is by using positive affirmations. The human brain is quite powerful, but it is susceptible to influence. You have more control over your brain than you believe. If you keep repeating the same thought, your brain starts accepting it as the truth. This is why negative self-talk is quite harmful. A simple way to put a positive spin on your thoughts is by using positive affirmations. Positive affirmations are positive statements created to subtly influence your mind. For instance, if you constantly tell yourself, "I cannot do this," or "I am not good enough," it will become a self-fulfilling prophecy. Instead of such negative thoughts, start using positive affirmations such as, "I am open to all of life's experiences, I am proud of myself and my abilities," or "I am in charge of what I do with my day today." You don't have to follow the same statements; tweak them according to the goals you are trying to achieve. Positive affirmations can be created in all aspects of life.

Once you have these affirmations in place, it is time to start practicing them. The key to rewiring your mind for positivity is repetition. Set aside 10 minutes to repeat the positive affirmations daily. Ideally, start your day with positive affirmations. You can also write them down and place them in easily visible locations around the house.

Reframe Negative Thoughts

With positive affirmations, you have the power to reframe all your negative thoughts. We are all constantly thinking about multiple things. All these thoughts are related to different aspects of your life and they can be both positive and negative. The problem with negative thoughts is, if you leave them unchecked, they can soon become overwhelming. This negative thinking prevents you from cultivating an attitude of positivity and gratitude. Instead of trying to push the negative thoughts away, start reframing them. Have you ever tried ignoring or pushing a specific thought away but it kept coming back? Did it feel like the thought became stronger than it was? The more you avoid thinking about a specific thought, the more potent the thought becomes. Avoid pushing the thought away and instead, replace it with something positive.

To do this, you need to become conscious of your thoughts. If you feel a negative thought creeping in, take a break and concentrate on reframing it. For instance, if you start thinking, "I cannot do this, I am not smart enough to do this," or "I don't think I will ever achieve my goals," it's time to put a positive spin on them. Instead of these negative thoughts, start thinking, "Even if I cannot do this right away, I know I can get it done eventually; I can work on improving my knowledge and skills to get things done," or "I'm proud of everything I have achieved so far and will keep moving toward success."

Reframing negative thoughts is not about avoiding, ignoring, or eliminating a thought. Instead, it's about shifting your perspective and putting a positive spin on it. When you start focusing on the negatives, you are essentially holding yourself back mentally. Whenever a negative thought steps into the picture, put a positive spin on it and try to find the motivation needed to tackle it. For instance, if you believe you cannot accomplish something, instead of thinking, "I cannot do it," replace it with, "I cannot do it yet." The addition of one word puts a positive spin on your internal dialogue.

Move On

Most of the negative thoughts we think are associated with the past. It's usually rumination about past events and circumstances that results in negative thinking. Whether it is a mistake, or regret over a missed opportunity, whatever happened in the past cannot be changed. So, what is the point of living in it? You have what it takes to create the future you desire. You cannot work on this future if you are still stuck in the past. For instance, if you are just getting out of a long-term relationship, you might harbor ill feelings toward your ex and relationships in general. You are entitled to feel and truly experience all emotions. There is nothing wrong with this. That said, you should also prepare yourself to move on. What will you obtain by living in the past? You will just end up feeling bitter and disappointed with others and yourself. In such situations, the best thing you can do is make your peace with the situation and work on creating a better future. Holding onto any bitter feelings toward your ex will make you feel bitter and lonely. It also increases the urge to indulge in self-pity. All this will not help you move on. By shifting your focus inward and concentrating on yourself, you can heal and move forward.

Another problem with not letting go of the past is it can influence your present. For instance, the inability to let go of a past relationship can sabotage your existing ones. When this happens, you are not only squandering the time available right now, but are compromising your future too. So, make it a point to let go of your baggage and work on creating a better future. Forget about your past because it is not necessary. Learn the lessons life was trying to teach you; take all the possible steps to ensure you don't repeat those mistakes, and move on.

Visualization Helps

A simple way to ensure that your self-talk takes a positive turn is by using visualization. Visualization is the simple technique of reconditioning your brain for positivity. Think about a specific scenario and visualize how it will be once you achieve your goal, dreams, or complete a specific task. Visualize how your day would be if you were the kind of person you desire to be. By focusing on this positive image, you are automatically reconditioning your brain for positivity.

For instance, if you want to become an entrepreneur, imagine how you will feel after you have achieved this goal! What will you feel, what will you be doing, who will be around you, what will you be wearing? Try to make this image as detailed and descriptive as you possibly can. Your visualization should be such that it engages all your senses. When this happens, you are automatically concentrating on positive aspects instead of getting bogged down by negative ones. Whenever your motivation levels run low or negative self-talk creeps in, use this visualization to tackle them. By envisioning your journey and the result, creating plans to deal with difficulties and finding the motivation needed to tackle setbacks becomes easier.

Help Others

If you want to feel better about yourself, start helping others. Helping others doesn't mean you have to spend all your time, energy, and resources engaging in charity work. Helping others and being of service is often about small steps instead of significant contributions. It can be something as simple as helping a coworker with their extra workload during your free time or smiling at a stranger. You can even pay for someone else's groceries or coffee. All it takes is the desire to help others, and living a service-oriented life becomes easier. When you help others, you automatically feel better about yourself.

What do you do when someone smiles at you? Chances are you will return the smile immediately. This is an automatic response. Similarly, when you help others, you start feeling better about yourself knowing you have managed to add some meaning or value to someone else's life. Make it a habit to help at least one person daily. Take some time and think about the different ways in which you can help others. If you have any specific skills or knowledge about a topic, consider mentoring or teaching others. Even spreading information and knowledge is a form of service. The list is endless. The world we live in is filled with pain and suffering. All you need to do is keep your mind and heart open to all the opportunities that present themselves. Whenever you see someone in need of assistance, do your part. You don't have to solve the entire problem but helping them a little will also make a difference.

Live Healthily

Your mental and emotional wellbeing is closely associated with your physical health. When you take care of your body, you automatically feel better. How do you feel when you return to work after pulling an all-nighter? Now, how do you feel after you've managed to get 8-10 hours of sleep and are well rested? In the former scenario, you probably feel unmotivated and extremely tired while in the latter you feel energetic and pumped up. This is because your body is not a tireless machine and taking care of it is your responsibility. By concentrating on consuming a healthy diet, getting enough rest, and exercising regularly, you are living a healthier life. Taking care of your physical health is the first step toward improving your mental and emotional well-being.

When you become physically active, your stress reduces, anxiety reduces, creativity increases and your self-confidence improves. Exercising regularly releases feel-good hormones known as endorphins in your body. These endorphins counteract the harmful effects of the stress hormone known as cortisol. In a way, you are automatically changing your mood by exercising.

Don't Stop Dreaming

An important aspect of letting go of negative self-talk is to never stop dreaming. If you stop, you are essentially preventing yourself from creating the future you desire. When you know you have something better to look forward to, your motivation increases. It also creates an attitude of positivity. So, regardless of what you do, never stop dreaming.

Understanding the Fear of Failure

We are all scared of failure. This fear can be immobilizing and incredibly powerful too. It can be so powerful that it surpasses our desire to be successful and will eclipse the motivation needed to become successful. If you are constantly scared about doing things incorrectly or are insecure about making mistakes, you cannot get much done. Fear is an undeniable part of human nature. Whenever you are attempting something different, fear steps into the picture. If you want to grow, keep trying different things. Fear is an unavoidable part of life. Instead of giving in to this fear, it is better to create a plan of action to fight it. Perhaps the worst fear that holds you back from creating the life you desire is that of failure. It is okay to be scared but you shouldn't avoid any of your fears. The trouble starts when you start letting emotions get the better of you.

If you are scared of failure, you start avoiding all situations that result in change. This fear also increases self-doubt, prevents you from making any progress, and reduces your ability to live in sync with your core values. It can also prevent you from trying altogether. Before you learn to overcome this fear, it is important to understand what causes it. The most common reasons are perfectionism, lack of self-confidence, a fragile sense of self-confidence, and over-personalization. When you start aiming for perfection in everything you say and do, the chances of getting anything done reduce. Similarly, if you over-personalize failures and setbacks, they prevent you from seeing the possibilities that lie beyond them. It also reduces the chances of leveraging any opportunities that come your way. If you are scared of change and avoid risks, you cannot grow. The primary reason for this is a false sense of self-confidence. If your self-confidence is based on the results you achieve instead of believing in your abilities, the fear of failure can become paralyzing.

Perhaps the most damaging effect of the fear of failure is it prevents you from taking on new challenges and risks. If you want to grow and progress, you need to constantly change and challenge yourself. If you don't keep challenging yourself, it develops an attitude of complacency. When you become complacent in your life, the chances of growth and progress reduce dramatically. After all, there is a direct relationship between risk and reward. If you don't take any risks, do not expect any rewards. That said, you should always focus on taking calculated risks instead of being impulsive. Impulsiveness is seldom desirable and is often more damaging than helpful. Learn to regulate your impulses and make good decisions.

If you are scared of failure, your motivation levels also reduce. In turn, making it doubly difficult to work on any goals you want to achieve or get started on new projects. If something seems extremely challenging or involves learning, many don't even get started because they are scared of failing. If you need to learn something new, it takes time and effort. Whenever you're learning something, failure is common. Have you ever seen babies taking their first steps? They tend to stumble and fall, but don't give up. You need to have a similar determination to keep going instead of being afraid to fail.

Apart from motivation, the fear of failure also reduces your self-esteem. The risk of engaging in negative self-talk increases due to this fear. It, in turn, reduces your self-confidence. When you indulge in excess negative self-talk, your self-confidence takes a beating and your self-esteem is automatically affected. This makes it difficult to work on your goals. This further reduces your self-esteem and increases negative self-talk. The fear of failure creates a vicious cycle of negativity and breaking free of it is not easy.

Any act or thought that effectively sabotages the good in your life is known as self-sabotage. You are your worst critic and enemy. The simplest way to avoid self-sabotage is by tackling the fear of failure. When you believe you cannot do something or think the outcome will not be favorable, the urge to succeed also reduces. This is nothing but an example of self-sabotaging behavior.

Another drawback of this fear is it increases any shame you experience. Knowing that you missed out on an opportunity because you were scared can induce feelings of worthlessness. When you fail, you might feel hopeless. To prevent these feelings, you automatically avoid all things which you believe will fail. To protect yourself from potential regret or disappointment, you are compromising on several things. This creates internal guilt and shame.

Ensure you don't miss out on any valuable opportunities that come your way; you need to keep yourself open to all challenges. The fear of failure can also reduce your chances of success. For instance, if you are used to doing well in life, the pressure to do better increases. This pressure can be internal or external. A high-achieving student is expected to keep performing better in school and achieve academic excellence. When this happens, the stress the student is experiencing automatically increases. After all, failure in such instances means disappointing others as well. For them, failure becomes unthinkable. It also becomes nightmare-inducing content for the brain. If you are used to success or you believe others expect you to succeed, the fear of failure becomes real. It becomes extremely frightening. In such instances, chances are you start overworking, and stick to a brutal schedule because you are worried about failing. It also increases the risk of burnout. When this happens, your overall productivity automatically reduces.

Overcoming the Fear of Failure

Overcoming a fear is possible, only if you want to overcome it. To overcome this fear of yours, follow the practical suggestions discussed in this section.

Understand the Reason

If you want to overcome your fear, it's important to understand where it stems from. Understanding the root of the fear gives you power over it. Try to understand that your fear is usually worse in your head than it actually is. By understanding the reason or the source of this fear, you can finally face it head-on. For instance, you might be scared of failure because you aim for perfection. Some are scared of failure because of childhood patterns. Growing up in a household where validation is associated with success can be quite stressful. Unfortunately, this pattern sticks with you even in adulthood. Now that you understand the reason for your fear, dealing with it becomes easier. On the other hand, if you are scared of failure because you were taught to aim for perfection, you know the problem here too. The first step of problem-solving is to acknowledge the problem.

Reframe the Goal

When you hold onto an all-or-nothing attribute, you will be left with nothing in certain circumstances. It is important to have a clear vision or a goal in mind. That said, the goal should be such that it helps you learn something new. The chances of failure reduce when there is room for growth, improvement, and learning. Keep experimenting and innovating because you never know what might work. Even an idea that doesn't seem good right now might be quite effective when you implement it. Certain ideas might not pan out how you desire. The outcome doesn't matter in either situation because it gives you a chance to learn and grow. As long as you are aware of the ultimate goal, you can create a mindset which helps you take failure in a positive stride.

Positive Thinking

Your internal dialogue matters more than you believe. It essentially regulates how you feel about yourself, life in general, and influences your reactions and behaviors. We live in a world obsessed with success. Due to this, most of us forget that failure is also a part of the journey. For instance, did you know that Walt Disney was fired from a newspaper job because they believed he was not creative enough? Well, he is the founder of the most famous animation studio in the world!

To overcome the fear of failure, you need to consciously work on changing your internal narrative. Instead of believing failure to be the end of the road, think of it as a learning opportunity. This will help you move forward. Start paying extra attention to your internal dialogue and use the suggestions discussed in this book to cultivate positive self-talk.

Worst-Case Scenario

To overcome the fear of failure, you need to think about the worst-case scenario. This might sound counterintuitive. After all, if you are trying to move ahead and stop being scared of failure, what's the point in thinking about the worst that can happen? Well, when you think about the worst outcomes, it gives you a chance to prepare for different situations. Use visualization to overcome the fear of failure. Visualization is the simple act of picturing how the future might turn out to be. In some cases, if the worst-case scenario comes true, it can be devastating. On the other hand, there will be plenty of scenarios where even if something bad happens, it doesn't mean the end of the world. Therefore, it's important to consider how you view your worst-case scenarios.

Unfortunately, a common mistake most of us make is that we give scenarios and circumstances more power than they deserve. When you do this, you are consciously giving away your power to an external factor out of your control. Instead of all this, the best thing is to understand that failure is never permanent. For instance, if you are getting started on your entrepreneurial journey, it will be a learning experience. Be prepared for an upward learning curve. All the business decisions you make might not pan out and understand that any challenge you experience will only be temporary. You can always change your strategy to work on improving yourself and the business. In such instances, the worst-case scenario is that your business comes to an end. If that happens, what can you do? By asking yourself this question and considering the alternatives, dealing with the scenario becomes easier if it manifests.

Use Visualization

Life is quite unpredictable so when you have already thought about specific outcomes in a given situation, you are better prepared to deal with them. By mentally preparing yourself for a challenge, it becomes easier to face it, if it manifests. This also reduces potential risks and the chances of failure. For instance, you might be worried about shifting to a new city or taking a new job. In such instances, carefully think about all the positive and negative aspects of the decision you want to make. This gives you a chance to determine the potential failures and successes you will encounter due to your decision. This gives you better clarity about what you can expect regardless of whether it's good or bad. So, if the worst comes true, you are already prepared to deal with it.

Have a Backup Plan

Having a backup plan is a great practice. If your worst-case scenario comes true, you need to know what to do. Instead of catastrophizing about whatever has happened, it's better to prepare and have a plan to implement. Remember to always prepare for the worst but hope for the best. A backup plan also increases your self-confidence and gives you the courage required to take on calculated risks and more challenges. For instance, if you want to become an entrepreneur and have applied for a loan to start your business, what is the worst-case scenario here? Perhaps your loan is rejected or you don't acquire the required funds to get going. In such instances, what can you do? If you have a backup plan to raise funds, then tackling the situation if it occurs becomes easier. This also gives you the courage to take on the risk of becoming an entrepreneur. Once you get started, dealing with any challenge that comes your way becomes easier because you have a plan in place.

Learn Your Lessons

If you want to truly succeed and discover your potential, it's important to keep learning and growing. The minute you stop learning, you stop growing. To overcome the fear of failure, you need to start learning your lessons. Whenever you fail or are rejected, life is trying to teach you an important lesson. Unless you learn this lesson, you keep repeating the mistake. Learn from every situation even if it doesn't seem ideal to you right now. If you learn from failure, you start viewing the experience as an opportunity for growth and development. This, in turn, will change your attitude about failure.

Remember, you don't have to feel overwhelmed and you certainly don't have to do everything at once. Instead, take things one step at a time. By doing this, overcoming your fear becomes easier. Once you see the positive effects of letting go of this fear, tackling it and keeping it at bay becomes easier. Always understand that failure is nothing but an opportunity to grow and develop. Instead of worrying about the outcome, concentrate on doing your best.

Empowering Lessons to Learn from Failure

Unless you learn to take failure in stride, you cannot achieve success. There is no reason to believe failure means you cannot succeed. Remember, success doesn't happen overnight. All that matters is your perspective. There is empowerment in failure and it can be transformed into success. Here are different lessons you can learn from failure in any aspect of your life.

The first lesson is that failure is not forever. Whenever you are dealing with challenging circumstances or experience failure, you might think it is permanent. The good news is that nothing in life is permanent. When you embrace all challenges, you will realize failure doesn't last forever. The only thing that matters is your attitude. You can always get back on your feet, provided you want to. You can also try your hand at something easier to regain confidence and motivation to keep going.

No one is immune to failure. Even those who are successful encounter failure at one point or another. So, failure is not unique and it is not restricted to you. It might feel as if nothing is working out, and the deck is stacked against you. The only thing you must remember is how you deal with failure because it is an inevitability. There will be different reasons why you did not accomplish the outcome you desire. In such instances, all you need to do is take time for self-introspection and understand where you went wrong. Learn your lessons without making the same mistakes in the future, and keep going.

While dealing with failure or rejection, it might seem overwhelming. It can be all-consuming to the extent that it becomes the only aspect of your life you are concentrating on. Remember, even things that seem important right now will change. The failure which is paralyzing you right now might be forgotten tomorrow, provided you want to move on. Chances are, you have experienced situations in the past that seemed extremely important at a given point but no longer matter. For instance, when in school, exams might have seemed like the only important aspect of life. Once you start working, you'll realize there's so much more to life than just studying. With time, our perspective toward ourselves and the world starts changing. This results in a change of priorities. If your priorities change, your attitude about failure also changes.

When failure stems from an external source, it becomes difficult not to take it personally. It is not a shortcoming. Don't let your confidence take a backseat because you believe the failure reflects poorly on your character or competence. Instead, it's simply an opportunity to learn and grow. By focusing on doing your best, making good decisions, and subconsciously improving yourself, dealing with failure becomes easier.

What others think of you is not your responsibility. The only person you are responsible for is yourself. How you view yourself and life, in general, determines your ability to succeed. If you start worrying about what others think or feel, you cannot accomplish anything. So, stop worrying about others. Remember, even if you are criticized, it doesn't have to be the truth. Truth is quite subjective and changes from one individual to another. Instead of judging yourself, distance yourself from the criticism; view it from a neutral perspective and consider all the changes you can make. This promotes corrective action and gives you a positive direction to work on.

Rejection is incredibly powerful. Have you ever noticed that most success stories are about people who have managed to overcome different adversities in life? Anything that does not kill you only makes you stronger. Overcoming adversities and facing rejection brings you a step closer to success. So, view all adversities in life as a tool for self-improvement. You can turn adversity into a winning situation, provided you want to.

An important lesson life tries to teach you in the form of failure is patience. You cannot succeed overnight. Also, you cannot succeed without failing. When you become patient and resilient, you keep trying regardless of the outcome. This increases your chances of success. Patience is a valuable virtue but is seldom focused on these days. We live in a world where most of us desire instantaneous results. When you don't get such results immediately, you become disappointed. Instead, believe that there is something better in store for you and concentrate on creating the future you desire.

Training and practice are crucial in life. When you train and prepare yourself to deal with different circumstances, dealing with them and their outcomes becomes easier. The same is applicable for rejection as well. Whenever you are dealing with rejection, think of it as the quickest way to immunize yourself. Once you are immune to rejection, you concentrate on efforts instead of outcomes. Unfortunately, whenever we face any challenges or rejections, most of us start engaging in negative self-talk. Instead, stay calm and concentrate on your performance. Look for ways to improve yourself and avoid the same mistake in the future.

Failure teaches humility. Humility is needed to see the bigger picture in life. Understand that we are all part of something bigger. There is no such thing as a small action. Everything you do, regardless of how big or small it seems, matters in the end. It teaches you to become humble. Failure teaches you that you are not invincible. It presents all your flaws, weaknesses, and shortcomings. Once you are aware of this, improving yourself becomes easier. If you think you are invincible, you stop looking for avenues to change. Without change, you cannot move ahead or grow. This results in stagnation instead of growth.

While dealing with challenging circumstances in life, your self-confidence can take a hit. The best thing you can do in such situations is to take action. Instead of wallowing in self-pity or worrying about failure, it is better to redirect your mental faculties. Concentrate on everything you can do and the steps you can take. When you take action, your ability to think positively improves. This also prevents stagnation. When you start prioritizing action over thoughts, you can cover more distance regardless of all the hurdles you face. So, start doing it!

Secrets of Turning Failure into Success

There is no reason to believe failure is the end of the road. If you want to start living your life without fearing failure, you have essentially learned one of the secrets to success. Learning to turn your failures into success will set you apart from others and make you unstoppable. If you learn something whenever you fail and turn it into a success, no one can stop you. To do this, here are some secrets you should know about changing your attitude related to success and failure.

How you think matters a lot because it influences your perspective toward life. You need to understand what success and failure mean to you. Most of us view success and failure on a scale where each lays on the extreme end. Black and white thinking or an all-or-nothing perspective means many believe they have either succeeded or failed. If they don't succeed, they automatically assume they have failed. This black and white thinking will not get you far in life. Instead of viewing failure and success on the spectrum, think of it as two sides of the same coin. What if you can turn failure into success and move ahead? Instead of viewing failure as the worst-case scenario or the end of the road, think of it as a stepping-stone. Remind yourself that success lies ahead of failure. If success is your destination, failure is a pit stop along the way. By simply shifting how you view success and failure, your ability to deal with it improves.

Make Peace with Failure

Whenever you fail, you are presented with an incredible opportunity to learn a valuable lesson. Whether it's a failed relationship or not getting the desired grade in school, these are all opportunities to learn, grow, and develop. So, start viewing failure as a learning opportunity. By using this logic, the more you fail and the quicker you do it, the chances of success increase drastically. It might sound counterintuitive, but this reverse thinking helps a lot. Instead of aiming only for success, make your peace with failure. Learn your lessons, cut your losses, and move on.

Rejoice Failures

Whenever you succeed or win, you tend to celebrate. But, it's not just about celebrating your success; start celebrating your losses too. It's okay if you don't win. When you start celebrating your losses, you are taking them positively. Instead of letting them hold you back, you are doing whatever you can do to move ahead. Don't punish yourself mentally for not succeeding. Don't feel guilty for not getting the results you desire and certainly don't engage in negative self-talk. Instead, do yourself a favor and start focusing on what you want to achieve. Even if you have failed now, it just means you are a step closer to success. This is a reason worth celebrating so start rejoicing your failures too.

Setting "No" Goals

We all want to succeed and this attitude usually reflects in how we establish goals. Start establishing 'no' goals. This does not mean you are not creating a goal. Instead, it means you are creating goals where you are told no. For instance, a salesperson might establish a 'no' goal of 20. If the salesperson had a goal of converting two prospects or getting two people to say yes to them, they would stop making an effort as soon as they hit this number. Now, if the first two people they tried to sell to agree, and turn into paying customers, their job ends there. If the salesperson concentrates on a 'no' goal of 20, their job doesn't end until they have heard 'no' from 20 prospects. When they do this, the chances of getting more people who would say 'yes' increases due to the wider pool. If you have 'yes' goals, your progress and acceleration slow down as soon as you attain success. On the other hand, a 'no' goal keeps you on your toes. Even if someone says no to you, you don't think of it as a failure. You start viewing it as a desirable answer.

Work on Courage

If you want to take on new challenges in life, you need the self-confidence to move ahead. Without this confidence, you cannot take the required risks to try new things. Self-confidence stems from internal strength and courage. The good news is that courage is like a muscle. As with any other muscle, the more you exercise it, the stronger it gets. The same rule is applicable to your confidence and courage too. The simplest way to improve your self-confidence or courage is by dealing with fears. Face your fears instead of shying away from them. Stop avoiding them and tackle them head-on. Once you do this, your self-esteem and confidence immediately increase. Your courage muscle also becomes stronger whenever you take action instead of over analyzing and overthinking.

Talk to Others

Two heads are better than one when it comes to problem solving. If you are feeling stuck or are unable to solve a specific challenge or a problem, talk to others. Whether it's a friend, stranger, or acquaintance, sharing your problems with others opens your mind to different perspectives. Obtaining different perspectives changes how you view a given situation. While engaging in candid conversations with others, you are essentially thinking out loud. The simple act of saying your ideas out loud will help you think creatively. Some ideas might sound quite good but when you talk about them, you will realize the different loopholes they come with. Similarly, even a silly idea might be quite creative and exactly what you need when you share it with others.

Use a Mind Map

As with writing in a journal, creating a mind map is also a great way to strengthen your problem-solving skills. Start by writing down your problem in the center of a page. After this, start writing different ideas or solutions you have to solve the problem. For each idea or solution, make a note of its pros and cons. When you can see all the information laid out in front of you, it promotes creative thinking. This activity gives you a bird's eye view of where you are and where you want to go. It encourages cognitive thinking while actively engaging your senses.

Sleep on It

A simple yet effective means to think outside the box is by sleeping on an idea. Make a note of your problem if you feel stuck. Similarly, if you think you have had a breakthrough, write it down. After this, sleep on it. When you wake up after a good night's sleep, your brain will be decluttered and more active to think creatively. When you are well rested and refreshed, you will have a better sense of clarity. Remember, your brain is not a tireless machine and it needs to recuperate. By giving yourself a much-needed break, you are promoting creative thinking.

Talk to a Child

When in doubt, try explaining your problem to a child. This helps simplify the problem you are facing. By describing it in simple words, you get a better understanding of what you need, the steps to be taken, or even the mistakes you are making. Children are better at thinking outside the box than adults. Why don't you ask a child what they think of your idea? If nothing else, you will at least obtain honest feedback from them.

Mistakes to Avoid While Chasing your Dreams

In the previous chapters, you were told to dream big and keep chasing your dreams. You were also introduced to a variety of steps you can take to achieve those goals. That said, there are certain mistakes you must avoid while chasing your dreams. You don't always have to make mistakes to learn. There is a lot to be learned from mistakes others have made. Let's look at some common mistakes you should avoid.

The first mistake you shouldn't make is to expect quicker results. If you are concentrating on making a change or achieving a goal, remember it is not an overnight process. It takes patience, practice, consistency, effort, and dedication to achieve goals in life. If you expect fast results, you are setting yourself up for disappointment. This disappointment will prevent you from taking any action in the future. It also increases feelings of frustration. So, do yourself a favor and stop expecting immediate results. While working on your goals or dreams, never underestimate the importance of patience.

Whatever you do, do not view failure as a sign to give up. Just because things haven't gone your way doesn't mean you should stop trying. It's been repeatedly stressed that you should stop being scared of failure. That said, even if you face failure, do not give up. It simply means you need to change your approach or come up with a better plan to deal with the situation. If you give up the moment you fail, you cannot achieve your goals. When in doubt, ask yourself what you can do differently to move on from your failure. Consider if any specific situation or factor might have changed in your life that prevented your success. Another suggestion you can use is to place yourself in someone else's shoes and view the situation from their perspective.

If you want to achieve your goals, be prepared for the daily grind. The daily grind is not always exciting but is needed to achieve the results you desire. Consistency is crucial for success. At times, you need to perform the same actions repeatedly to achieve your goals. This can become boring. Instead of getting bored, derive pleasure from the routine activities if you want to become successful. For instance, a successful athlete will keep training and practicing on perfecting one skill for months and years on end. This is the same motivation you need to achieve your goals.

Not planning is equivalent to planning to fail. If you want to achieve your goals, ensure you have plans for the unexpected. While chasing your goals in life, start expecting the unexpected. This is the only way you can rise above different challenges or obstacles you will face along the way. If you aren't prepared for the unexpected, you will be caught off-guard. This also results in the waste of resources. Apart from that, it can also shake your self-confidence. To avoid all this, simply prepare yourself for different circumstances and outcomes.

Do not get distracted by others or life events while chasing your dreams and goals. Ensure that you are focusing only on one goal at a time. Once you have achieved one thing, you can move on to the next. If you try to do multiple things at once, you will get nothing done. Multitasking reduces your overall productivity and efficiency. Unfortunately, we live in a world that glorifies multitasking. Remember, the resources available at your disposal will be scarce but they will have multiple uses. Unless you learn to make the most of such resources you cannot be successful. For instance, your ability to concentrate and think creatively is a resource too. If you are thinking about multiple goals or problems at once, you cannot think clearly. Instead, it will simply result in accumulation of mental clutter. So, avoid multitasking. Do not get distracted by others, their views and opinions, or any other goal. Focus only on one thing at a time and achieving your dream will become easier.

It's repeatedly mentioned that you need to plan to achieve your goals. However, if your planning is unrealistic, you cannot achieve said goals. For instance, if you think you can train for twenty hours on any given day, you are planning for disappointment. Be realistic while making a note of all the different steps you will need to execute to achieve your goal. This is the only way to move ahead. If the steps you need to take are unrealistic or impossible, the goal will automatically become impossible.

Chapter 5:
Your Value, Your Mental Well-Being

There is so much more to life than success. Emotional intelligence, integrity, honesty, forgiveness, love, mental peace, and even kindness are inner values that are equally important. However, success is the only one we focus on. We live in a world that places too much emphasis on outward appearances and superficiality instead of things that really matter. This tends to create a notion of success that is solely based on outward appearances. This can severely harm your sense of self-worth. For instance, if you start believing you are not successful unless you own the most luxurious car or purchase a big house, you are setting yourself up for failure. This also creates frustration while reducing your self-worth.

By focusing purely on outward appearances, unnecessary comparisons are triggered. This comparison is not only unhealthy but is nothing more than self-sabotage. The only way to break free of this is by understanding your value. By concentrating on your self-worth, you can finally stop focusing on outward appearances. Remember, whenever you compare, you are not only engaging in negative self-talk but are being unfair to yourself too.

Take a moment and think about it. Have you ever used an external factor as a yardstick to determine your self-worth?

Now, think about how each of these criteria forces you to compare yourself to others or is based on seeking external validation. When you start using outward appearances to measure your success, your self-worth takes a backseat. It also increases stress, the risk of burnout, and frustration. When your self-worth comes from the inside, leading a happier and healthier life becomes a possibility.

Understanding Your Value

To understand your true value, it's important to understand you are not a reflection of what others think or believe. Remember, in life, we are all entitled to our perspectives. Our perspectives are widely different due to different circumstances including our upbringing and life experiences. So, why should you judge yourself based on how others view you?

Your value is not influenced by how others view you. For instance, if you believe value is associated with monetary success, you will automatically believe only those with money are valuable. According to this line of thought, those who aren't wealthy aren't valuable. The paradox of valuing outward appearance is quite real. If you take a moment to consider, you will realize the people you idealize the most are the other ones you are jealous of. You are jealous of their success and the lives they are living. Just because someone seems to fit your definition of success doesn't mean they are successful. When the feeling of success stems from the inside, no one can take it away.

You will also become unstoppable when you understand your value.

To understand your value, here are some practical suggestions you can use.

You need to start believing that you have the required skills to achieve the success you desire. You need to believe you are passionate about the things you are doing. You need to believe you are special and unique. Start believing that you have the power to execute and achieve your goals. When you start living your life believing in yourself, you will see a positive change.

You need to understand that your potential is incredibly valuable. If you don't value yourself, you will never understand or even appreciate your potential. Unless you understand your potential, you cannot understand your self-worth. If you cannot do this, you cannot understand what you are truly capable of achieving. The thing about potential is, it is intangible. It's more about your mindset than anything else. Your ability to achieve success improves when you have a positive mindset. Similarly, a negative mindset prevents you from leveraging any opportunities that present themselves in life. Remember, your value is not determined by where you are right now. Instead, it's about where you want to go and how you manage to get there. Your self-worth reduces when you ignore your potential. Take some time and consider your strengths instead of focusing only on your weaknesses.

Most of us are incapable of understanding our self-worth because we focus too much on criticism. You are your worst critic. This is one of the reasons why self-sabotage is quite easy. How you treat yourself determines how you feel. If you have a positive attitude about yourself and believe you are valuable, your self-confidence, self-esteem, and independence increase. If you treat yourself poorly, it automatically sends a message to others that they can get away with treating you the same. Unless you see your self-worth, you cannot expect it from others.

If you are struggling to understand your strength, take some time for self-introspection. Think about different challenges you have managed to overcome. These challenges don't have to be anything significant. Every little hurdle or obstacle you face in life teaches you something about yourself. Whether it's resilience or honesty, these are all important values. Another simple technique is to talk to your loved ones. You can ask your family members, partners, colleagues, or even friends about your strengths. There might be certain things about yourself you have never paid attention to but others did. Chances are you have undervalued yourself. Since we all have different perspectives, asking others for feedback will open you up for better insights. You can use this feedback to change your perspective about yourself.

To understand your value, think about your passions. Whatever you are passionate about automatically adds value to your life. Find and pick a goal you are passionate about. By focusing on your passions, you are automatically living a meaningful life. Apart from this, another important part of understanding your value is to stop associating it with monetary success. Your value should never stem from external sources. If this happens, your value depreciates the moment the external factor goes away. Instead, it stems from the inside. By shifting your focus and attitude toward yourself, your ability to see your self-worth improves.

Learn to be Fearless

Fears aren't restricted to just failure. We all have different fears and they are quite a common emotion. The problem starts when you let the fear get in the way of your life. If your fears are preventing you from living and doing what you love, it is time to become fearless.

Remember, becoming fearless doesn't mean you have no fears. Instead, it's about rising above your fears and preventing them from regulating your life. It's about being in control of your fears instead of letting them decide your fate. The first step to becoming fearless is to accept your fear. After all, how can you solve a problem if you don't even accept its existence? It is okay to accept that you have fears. In fact, this only makes you human. Unless you accept the different fears harbored within, you cannot create a plan of action to overcome them. While doing this, it's always better to make a note of your fears instead of believing you can think things through. When you write them down, the fear loses power over you. Remember, your fears are always worse in your head than they actually are. With this in mind, let's learn to become fearless.

Ask yourself why you want to overcome a specific fear. Unless you are internally motivated to tackle the fear, you cannot change anything. In fact, this internal motivation is needed in all aspects of your life. Without this motivation, there is no reason why you should even make a change. Making a change is seldom easy and unless you have good reasons for it, you cannot go ahead and ensure it lasts. If you are struggling to understand why you want to overcome fear, visualize how your life will be once you are free of said fear. Consider how you want your future self to look—the fearless self. Try to make this visualization as realistic as you possibly can. This visualization will act as a motivating factor, especially when you don't feel like trying and want to give up.

If you want to become fearless, be willing to do silly things. Don't be scared of making a fool of yourself. You probably spend more time thinking about what others might be thinking about you than they actually do. This is human nature. We are constantly worried about being judged by others. Give yourself a break because no one is thinking about you as much as you believe they are. Instead of wasting your time doing this, it's better to go ahead and act silly. Once you are ready to risk the pain of making any mistakes, most of the fears you have harbored will go away.

Whenever you are working on overcoming your fears, ensure that you are objective and rational. Consider where the fear comes from and what you can do to alleviate it. Ask yourself whether the fear is based on reality or is caused due to someone else's opinions or thoughts. Ask yourself whether this fear is your own or someone else's. Unknowingly, we tend to imbibe other's fears and project them as if they are our own. If the fear is not even your own, why are you holding onto it? Why are you letting it guide your life?

It is never too late to learn anything in life. Find a teacher or a mentor who will guide and help you overcome your fears. Observe all the relationships and look for someone who always gives you clear directions and is brutally honest. You can use this honesty and opinions from others to overcome any fear you are facing. The said person can also help create a sense of accountability. This, in turn, increases the urge to follow through on your promises.

Whenever you feel scared or afraid, start replacing it with gratitude. For instance, if you are scared of public speaking, be grateful because you have an opportunity to connect with others. By concentrating on the positives or looking for the silver lining, you are shifting your focus away from the fear. When you stop focusing on the fear, its hold over you reduces naturally. This makes it easier to regain composure instead of letting the fear get the best of you.

It's human nature to instantly avoid anything that scares us. To overcome your fear, embrace the discomfort it comes with. Overcoming your fear is not an overnight process. It takes time, consistency, and dedication. Always remember you cannot gain anything in life if there isn't any pain involved in the process. When you embrace the struggle and work on improving yourself, the fear slowly goes away. Change is seldom easy, but the effort you make will be worth your while.

A simple way to tackle your fears is by sharing them with others. At times, our worries and fears are worse in our heads than they actually are. When you reach out to others and share your worries with them, you might obtain surprising insights about yourself. This might also help solve the problem at hand. You never know, you might connect with someone who is struggling with the same issues as you. The simple act of sharing your troubles with others also takes away any loneliness caused by your fears. When you start talking about it, the fear slowly loses its hold over you. Don't be worried about how others will perceive you if you share your fears. If others judge or ridicule you for your fears, it reflects poorly on them and not you.

Another brilliant technique you can use is to visualize how a fearless person would deal with the same situation as you. If you are scared of failure, ask yourself how a person who isn't scared of making mistakes would deal with the given situation. Once you have the answer, start replicating their behaviors. This helps put things in perspective. By creating an image of fearlessness in your mind, you are conditioning your brain to let go of the fear. At times, the idea of faking it until you make it also helps. Your mind is powerful, but it is susceptible to manipulation too.

Whenever you are trying to overcome a fear, you need to free yourself. Stop believing you need to be in control of every situation in life. This is not only impossible but impractical too. Life is unpredictable and regardless of how hard you try, there will be several external factors beyond your control. Instead of holding tight onto this dire need for control, relinquish it. Once you do this you will realize there are plenty of scopes to open up and develop.

Stop letting your fears get the best of you. You are so much stronger than you believe. If it feels like your fears are preventing you from living the life you desire, there is no time like the present to work on relinquishing them.

Chapter 6:
Self-Love is an Action

Life is filled with challenges, obstacles, and failures. Whether you deal with them or succumb to them determines if you are living a meaningful life or not. If you want to understand your potential, don't let challenges paralyze you. Regardless of how overwhelming or intimidating a challenge seems, you have the power to overcome it. You can rise up, and shine, but the choice is yours.

Don't Run Away from Problems

It is quite easy to run away from a problem or ignore it instead of solving it. Facing a problem is seldom easy. A primary reason we avoid our problems is that they are uncomfortable. Our brains are wired to avoid any situation that causes discomfort. However, you cannot be successful unless you learn to face your problems. Let's look at different suggestions you can use to avoid running away from your problems and instead, learn to face them.

Whenever you are running away from a problem, you are essentially taking the easy way out. Running away might work for the time being, but it does not solve your problem. How long or far can you run? Regardless of the distance you cover, the problem doesn't go away. Sooner or later, you need to face it. It's always better to face the problem immediately instead of letting it manifest into something bigger. This act by itself can make a seemingly simple problem quite complicated and overwhelming. A simple way to deal with your problem is to understand that all problems don't have solutions. You don't have to constantly look for solutions; instead, just letting things be the way they are for a while will help. At times, when you are in a rush to solve a problem, the solution might not come to you. Regardless of how hard you try, the solution seems to elude you. In such situations, the best thing you can do is wait for a while. You might even stumble upon the solution once you stop focusing too much on it.

.

When you run away, instead of resolving an issue, you are picking up more things to do. For instance, you have a project due at work, but have run into an issue. Unless you solve the issue, you cannot move ahead. However, the issue seems overwhelming or scary, so you take on another project. The same situation repeats. So, ultimately, you have simply increased your workload, haven't attained any results, and are just running away from the problem. This increases your burden and workload. In the end, things become more stressful than they need to be. When you are stressed, solving a problem also becomes difficult. So do yourself a favor and instead of running away from your problems, take a moment to think about where they stem from. Looking at the root cause of the problem helps understand where you are going wrong.

To stop running away from your problems, you need to become courageous. Start embracing suffering and discomfort, and dealing with the problem becomes easier. This might sound counterintuitive, but it works. For instance, if you want to become more energetic, increase your stamina, and become strong, you need to let go of unhealthy eating habits even though they are momentarily pleasurable. It means you need to work hard, exercise regularly, sleep on time, and cultivate healthy habits. Doing this will cause some discomfort. However, it helps rectify a problem. Once you understand there is a certain degree of suffering involved in solving a problem, dealing with the circumstances becomes easier. Accepting the fact that you will experience discomfort and suffer for a while will make things easier for you. When you accept that suffering is a part of growing, it gives you a chance to prepare yourself for it. This preparation makes it easier to deal with the circumstances when they occur. When you know what to expect, you can create a plan of action to reduce that discomfort.

Fear comes from not knowing. It's the uncertainties in life that cause fear. It also stems from the lack of knowledge. Fear is also a reason why many avoid facing their challenges and instead choose to run away. The simplest way to deal with such fears is by equipping yourself with more information. The best way to do this is by establishing short and long-term plans for yourself. Set some goals, create a plan of action to achieve those goals, and start implementing the plan. While doing this, you are automatically forced to think about different setbacks, flaws, or loopholes in your plan. This prepares you for the uncertainties while giving you the confidence needed to deal with the problems or challenges.

When it feels like you are surrounded by problems, or life has become too overwhelming, remind yourself that you are not alone. You are never alone. There will be others who are sailing in the same boat as you. Reaching out to them, talking to your loved ones, and depending on your support system in times of need makes it easier to face any challenges that come your way.

A common reason why many try to run away from their problems is that they lack self-belief and self-confidence. If you think you are not capable of tackling your challenges, you will look for different ways to avoid or run away from them. When you feel confident, you take action regardless of all the worries or fears you might harbor. You start realizing the need to do something and unless you try, you'll never know. Start believing in yourself because you're capable of tackling all the different challenges that life throws your way. Self-confidence and self-belief need to come from within. By letting go of any mental blockages preventing you from moving ahead, dealing with problems becomes easier.

Take some time for rest. Never overlook the importance of taking breaks. It is not just your body that needs rest, your mind also needs to relax. Depriving yourself of this relaxation will result in burnout sooner or later. We tend to run away from our problems when we feel burdened. So, taking your mind off your problems and concentrating on enjoyable and relaxing activities will make you calmer. This also reduces the risk of burnout. By giving yourself a break between tasks, you can ensure you don't lose any momentum and are instead actively solving all problems that come your way.

Running away from your problem does not involve any movement or momentum whatsoever. Instead, it simply keeps you stuck in the current situation. If you want to achieve success and become unstoppable, you need to gain a little momentum. How can you gain this momentum? The only way is to start concentrating on taking small steps daily. If you are faced with a problem, look for different ways to solve it. Once you have a plan in place, start implementing it. Every little step or positive action that helps solve your problem—even if it's only by a small proportion—gives you the motivation required to keep going. This helps build the momentum needed to tackle the impossible.

All meaningful changes in life are based on a single choice you make. You cannot make a change unless you take a stand for yourself. Unless you realize that change is needed, you cannot deal with your problems. It doesn't matter how fast or far you run. Your problems will catch up with you sooner or later. So, at one point or another, you need to put your foot down and decide how you want to address the problem. You need to make this choice regardless of the costs involved. You need to have some strength and resilience to do this.

Practicing Self-Love

If you want to understand your strengths, discover your potential and rise up to life's challenges, you need to start loving yourself. Remember love and compassion aren't restricted to others. You need to love yourself too. Unless you do this, you cannot expect it from anyone else. You need to be your own cheerleader, supporter, and motivator. After all, true happiness stems from within. Unless you are happy with yourself, you cannot move ahead in life. When you start practicing self-care and self-love, you automatically feel better about yourself. Regardless of what happens, you know you can count on yourself. Knowing this can make you feel quite good. Let's look at practical suggestions you can use to practice self-love daily.

Avoid Comparison

If you want to feel better about yourself, one habit you need to avoid is comparison. Humans are social beings and are naturally competitive. This competition triggers the urge to compare yourself with others. When you start doing this, you are breeding dissatisfaction and contempt. Apart from making yourself feel miserable, you will get nothing out of comparing yourself with others. Remember, you are unique and there is no one else like you on this earth. Instead of wasting your precious energy concentrating on others, direct it inward. Concentrate on yourself and the journey you want to take or the success you want to achieve.

Stop Focusing on Appearances

An important realization all women need to come to is understanding their value is not determined by their looks or appearances. This is crucial. Unfortunately, most of us have dealt with some form of discrimination based on our appearances at one point or another. Whether it's name-calling or criticism, when your value is associated with your looks, you will feel unmotivated. We have also internalized sexism to the extent that our appearance makes us feel inadequate. You are so much more than your looks. What is on the inside always counts and don't let anyone tell you otherwise. Stop equating your self-worth with your appearance, because beauty is just skin deep and looks fade. If you believe others will not accept or love you the way you are, perhaps reconsider the relationships in your life.

Don't Worry About Others

It's not just about comparing yourself to others, you should also stop worrying about others' opinions. Regardless of whether you are doing well or not, everyone will have an opinion about it. This is because we are different and have different perspectives, expectations, opinions, and ideas.

We are all entitled to have all these differences. That said, stop living your life because you're worried about what others might think or feel. You are not responsible for them. The only person you are responsible for is yourself. Stop wasting your time and energy trying to make everyone else happy. This is not only impossible but incredibly foolish too. While trying to do this, you will end up making the most important person unhappy—yourself.

Make Mistakes

We are not perfect and therefore, it's high time that we collectively normalize the concept of making mistakes. Mistakes are an important part of growing and developing in life. You cannot move ahead if you don't make any mistakes. Perfection does not exist and it's an illusion we are all chasing. For instance, you might need to work your way through several bad relationships until you find someone who truly appreciates you the way you are. By normalizing mistakes, we are taking away the stigma associated with them. This also reduces any stress you might be experiencing. So, it is okay to make mistakes. As long as you are learning from these mistakes and don't repeat them—it's all part of the progress that you are making.

Understand Your Fears

Feeling scared and harboring fears is quite natural. As with
making mistakes, accepting your fears is important.
Instead of rejecting your fears, acknowledge them, accept
them, and understand what caused them. This is a great
way of overcoming your fears and getting rid of them. By
spending some time on self-introspection, you can unmask
the issue causing your fears. When you know the reason,
tackling the fear and reducing any anxiety associated with
it also becomes easier.

Let Go of Toxicity

You don't need any negativity or toxicity in your life. Take
stock of all your relationships—personal and professional.
If you believe someone is hampering your progress or
preventing you from being yourself, you don't need such
relationships. It doesn't matter how close the person is to
you. If all they are doing is adding negativity and toxicity
to your life, get rid of them. If you cannot eliminate such
relationships, distance yourself from them. Don't be afraid
to break free of toxic relationships. Even though it might be
painful right now, it is good for your mental and emotional
well-being in the long run. After all, you are responsible
for yourself before anyone else.

Trust Yourself

You are smarter, stronger, and more empowered than you believe. So, trust yourself a little instead of trusting others. Listen to your gut instinct and follow your heart while making decisions. Trust yourself to make good decisions and your ability to make them will improve. Get in touch with what you want and understand yourself. After all, you're the only one who knows yourself. So, be your best friend, trust yourself, and do what you want to do.

Take Care of Yourself

Prioritize self-care. it is perfectly okay to put yourself before others. Unless you are taking care of yourself — physically, emotionally, and mentally, you cannot help others. If you are neglecting self-care because you're worried about what others might think, stop doing it right now. You are doing yourself a grave injustice by not taking care of yourself. Don't feel bad for putting yourself first. Women are accustomed and conditioned to putting others first. If such acts are harming your mental or emotional well-being, it's not worth it. Take the time needed to decompress, concentrate on your passions, and don't be scared to dream big.

Rule About Opportunities

If you want to get ahead in life, you need to make the best of each opportunity that comes your way. If it feels like there are no opportunities available right now, what is preventing you from creating new ones for yourself? There is no such thing as a perfect time or set up in life. Even if the setting isn't ideal right now, don't let it prevent you from reaching your goals and dreams. Learn to seize the moment because the time that goes by does not come back. Make the most of every moment you have right now because this truly is a gift.

Express Yourself

Don't hesitate or shy away from expressing your ideas, opinions, and views. You don't need someone else's permission to be yourself. Self-expression is an inherent right we are all blessed with and no one can take it away from you. Be comfortable in your own skin and start expressing yourself freely. Remember, self-expression doesn't mean hurting others. Instead, it's about joining a conversation, contributing your thoughts, and sharing your ideas or opinions without worrying about what others might think. Remember, your opinions and ideas are as important as someone else's and there is no reason why you shouldn't express yourself.

Feel Everything

Permit yourself to feel everything. You don't have to ignore or avoid your feelings or emotions. Get in touch with your true self. Don't judge your emotions as good or bad. Instead, let them flow freely. Understand what you want and expect in life. Once you are aware of all this, creating a life you have dreamed of becomes easier.

Treat Yourself

Is there something specific you've been meaning to buy but have put it on hold for one reason or another? Perhaps it's a gorgeous pair of designer shoes or a bag you've been eyeing for a while. Why don't you go ahead and treat yourself? You don't need a reason. You deserve to be pampered! As long as an occasional treat will not burn a hole in your pocket, there's no harm in enjoying life and having a little unplanned fun.

Schedule Fun Time

It might sound counterintuitive, but start prioritizing fun. Even if it means adding it to your daily to-do list or your calendar, go ahead and do it. Your fun time is as important as a doctor's appointment. You wouldn't cancel the latter and there is no reason why you shouldn't show the same commitment toward the former. Do not neglect your fun time or cancel it because you are flooded with work or are stuck with one commitment or another. Fun time is a commitment to yourself. When you start honoring the promises you made to yourself, you will feel better.

Stay Healthy

A simple way to start loving yourself is to take care of your health. It means you need to eat healthily, exercise regularly, get sufficient sleep at night, and take some time to relax. When you are mentally, physically, and emotionally healthy, taking on life's challenges becomes easier. Make it a point to exercise at least three times every week. Reduce your consumption of unhealthy processed and ultra-processed foods. Replace them with healthy and wholesome fruits, vegetables, lean protein, and unprocessed grains. Ensure that you get at least 6 hours of undisturbed sleep at night. Start making these simple changes to your daily routine and you will see a positive change.

There is Beauty Everywhere

If you want to feel better about yourself, start taking pleasure in all the small joys in life. Whether it's a healthy breakfast you eat in the morning or a pleasant conversation with a friend, these are incredible things. Make a note of everything you are grateful for and don't forget to thank the universe for the same. By taking joy in the little things in life, it will change your perspective for the better.

Chapter 7:
Face Your Fear and Rise to the Challenge

A famous quote by Thomas Edison says, "When you have exhausted all possibilities, remember this: you haven't!" The only way forward in life is to deal with your challenges instead of succumbing to them. By thinking outside the box, you can face your inner fears and rise to challenges.

Rise to the Challenge and Overcome It

When things aren't going your way, you will feel overwhelmed and it can be quite difficult to feel positive about anything. However, challenges are a part of life. There will be instances when you are facing the unexpected. This is not a reason to give up on your goals. Instead, you need to learn to rise to the challenge and overcome it to move ahead. It is normal to feel scared, overwhelmed, and helpless while facing challenging circumstances. That said, with a little preparation, you can create simple coping mechanisms to deal with challenging circumstances. Here are some tips you can use to deal with stressful circumstances and conquer them instead of succumbing to challenges.

Whenever you are dealing with a challenge, you need to separate yourself from the situation. If not, you will end up blaming yourself for everything and anything that goes wrong. It also increases the risk of not truly understanding what is happening. Instead of getting overwhelmed and internalizing the problem, separate yourself from it. Take a step back, view it from a neutral perspective and analyze it logically. When you do this, the risk of self-blame reduces and instead, it becomes easier to solve the problem.

Remember, you should never quit even if you don't succeed. If the situation wasn't tough, it would not be considered a challenge. Even if you haven't accomplished anything while dealing with the challenge, it's better to keep trying instead of giving up. If you want to keep trying, you need to have sufficient reasons and internal motivation to keep going despite failure. Take some time to refocus and concentrate on achieving your goal instead of giving up.

While dealing with challenges, it is quite easy to indulge in self-doubt. If you keep doubting yourself, you will not get anything done. Instead of all this, start believing in yourself a little. Instead of getting overwhelmed when you face a challenge head-on, start wherever you can and concentrate on making small changes whenever possible. Small movements help build momentum that keeps you going. Never underestimate the importance of small changes or actions you take. In the end, they all add up and bring you closer to your goals and dreams.

Avoid Self-Doubt

If you find yourself constantly doubting and second-guessing everything you say and do, you cannot accomplish much in life. Self-doubt can also sabotage any progress you make. To avoid giving in to self-doubt, follow these tips.

The human mind has an affinity for all things familiar. Even if the thing it is familiar with is sabotaging your happiness or success, your mind doesn't mind. The human mind seems to function on the concept of "it's better to be with the devil you know instead of the one you don't." This is why those with negative internal self-talk subconsciously prefer negative thinking. If your inner critic is quite loud, you get accustomed to the nagging feeling of not being good enough. To let go of self-doubt, you need to make the unfamiliar familiar to your mind. While you do this, you should simultaneously make the familiar seem unfamiliar. You can start using positive affirmations to recondition your mind to think positively. Whenever your internal critic says you are not good enough or sufficient, remind yourself that you are sufficient and enough the way you are. Keep repeating this phrase and your mind will start accepting it. Spend at least five minutes daily practicing different positive affirmations. This helps reprogram your mind and let go of internal self-doubt.

How you feel about yourself in any given situation is based on two things. The first factor is how you visualize the situation in your head and the second factor is your self-talk. Regardless of how unpredictable life is, you have complete control over your responses and reactions in any given situation. It is entirely up to you how you want to deal with the circumstances. Instead of relying on negative self-talk, it's better to replace self-doubt with something more positive. Whenever you feel self-doubt stepping into the picture, you have the power to regulate it by selecting words and images that make you feel better. By creating and maintaining a positive internal dialogue, dealing with the situation becomes easier.

The human brain is incredibly powerful and you have complete control over it. It is the most powerful weapon in your arsenal. You can use it to get what you want. Your mind tends to work against you when you don't know what you want, leaving it up to its own devices. Remember, you need to control it instead of letting it control your life. If you let your insecurities get the best of you, self-doubt will creep in. Remember you need to regulate what your mind tells you. Start engaging in positive self-talk and you will see that self-doubt slowly goes away.

Talk to yourself the way you would talk to a loved one. If you are constantly criticizing yourself or berating yourself for a mistake, ask yourself how you would deal with the situation if it was your loved one in your place. If your loved one came to you with a problem, how would you deal with them? Chances are you would be empathetic, compassionate, caring, and loving toward them. Now, you need to extend the same compassion toward yourself. Instead of berating yourself, give yourself a break. Avoid being harsh toward yourself, especially when you are already dealing with a problem.

Another simple way to let go of self-doubt is by concentrating on your past achievements. All the good you managed to achieve in the past and the good in your life right now are a sign that you aren't as bad as your inner critic says. In fact, this helps put things in perspective. All your achievements help build your case against self-doubt. By focusing on all your accomplishments, you are feeding your brain positive mental fodder.

Start Thinking Outside the Box

Chances are, you were told to start thinking outside the box by a teacher, parent, colleague, or even a manager at work. What does this mean? think creatively, critically, strategically, and concentrate on being innovative. The solution to your problem might not always be the common route used by others. At times, you need to step outside the box to solve your problems. Whenever it feels like you are succumbing to a challenge, remember that you have not thought outside the box yet. There is a way out of every situation, and all you need to do is look for it. This section will introduce you to simple suggestions that can be used to start thinking outside the box.

Understand the Reason

To think outside the box, ask yourself why you want to do this. What is the need or the reason to think outside the box? For instance, instead of thinking about how to solve a problem, ask yourself why you should solve it. Or, concentrate on all that you stand to gain by solving a specific problem. Instead of fixating on the problem and getting overwhelmed, it is better to think about the different benefits you stand to gain by solving said problem. This creates a positive shift in your perspective and makes it easier to solve the problem.

Clarity of Thoughts

To think outside the box, at times, you need to just stop thinking altogether. When your thoughts are running at 100 mph and you are entangled in a web of thoughts or ideas, it becomes difficult to see which ideas are truly viable. Simplify your thoughts, take a step back and try to view them. Instead of looking at all the thoughts at once, start with one thought and critique them individually. You can always add, eliminate, and expand upon the ideas you have. You cannot do all this if your head is cluttered with multiple thoughts. So, start with a little clarity, and finding a creative solution will become easier.

Use a Journal

A simple way to think outside the box is by writing down your thoughts. Take some time, grab a pen and paper, and let the words flow. You don't have to judge anything you have written right now. Whatever idea you have, write it down. Once you have written everything your mind will automatically be decluttered. Once you have the ideas in place, you can start evaluating them one at a time. This is better than getting overwhelmed by looking at all the different thoughts in your head. Think of it as a brain dump. By starting with a clean slate, it becomes easier to understand where you are and what you want to do. This also gives you a chance to concentrate on your passions and how you can channel them to solve your problems.

Devil's Advocate

To think outside the box, play the role of devil's advocate. Start by thinking the opposite of what you are already thinking right now. It's quite easy to fall in love with your ideas, for the sole reason that you are the one who came up with them. If you already love the idea because it is yours, you have formed an opinion. This opinion acts as a constraint. So, start by refuting your thoughts. Look for potential problems, setbacks, or loopholes in your existing ideas. By doing this, you are forcing your brain to think more clearly about what you want to do. By forcing yourself to see the opposite perspective of the one you have assumed, you are opening up your mind to more possibilities. This helps the creative juices flow.

Meditation Helps

Have you ever had brilliant ideas or breakthroughs while taking a bath? This is because your mind is distracted from the problem and is instead concentrating on a specific activity. This is precisely how the concept of meditation works. Meditation helps calm your mind, put things into perspective, and break free from different worries. Whatever you are doing, take a break from it. Concentrate on your breathing for a couple of minutes and nothing else. Let your thoughts flow. Don't try to regulate them right now. When you start meditating, you are emptying your mind. This makes it easier to concentrate on ideas and solutions. When you are calmer, thinking logically and rationally becomes easier.

Start Learning

If you feel stuck, learn something else. Whether it is a new skill or you want to take a class to hone your existing skills—do it. When you start learning, your mind is distracted. This approach helps look at your problems differently. It, in turn, promotes out-of-the-box thinking. For instance, if you want to become an entrepreneur and launch your own business, taking a class about launching a website will help. This opens your mind to different opportunities available. When you consider all the options, thinking about solutions becomes easier.

Chapter 8:
To Go from Undervalued to Unstoppable and Extraordinary

You can live the life you desire. Stop letting others tell you cannot. Don't let circumstances define you. Instead, live your life like a champion. To do this, you need to stop underestimating your capabilities. Instead, develop a mindset that encourages you to never quit. Don't stop trying!

Behaviors to Become Unstoppable

Learning to become good at something is quite easy. You can even become elite with plenty of practice, patience, and effort. However, only a few truly become unstoppable and extraordinary. To become unstoppable, you must understand the only competition you have is yourself. Don't compete with anyone else and start comparing yourself to the person you want to become. All those who are unstoppable have specific behaviors that set them apart from everyone else. Let's look at some behaviors that will make you unstoppable.

Stop Thinking

It might sound counterintuitive that you need to stop thinking to become unstoppable. Think before you act but if all you do is think and don't take any action, you will never know what you are capable of. We are all aware of what we want to do and how to go about it. Now, you should check whether you are aware of your desires and how to achieve them. Once you are aware, acknowledging and accepting them are the next steps. When you know the answers to both these steps, what is stopping you from performing? Instead of simply analyzing and thinking, start acting.

When in doubt, listen to your gut and go with what your intuition says. Regardless of how well laid out a plan seems, there will always be improvement once you start thinking and analyzing it deeply. In the end, this plan will amount to nothing without implementation.

Learn to be Prepared

It might sound like a scout club motto to always be prepared. Learn to be prepared in all situations. This probably sounds tricky, especially given the fact that life is unpredictable. If life is unpredictable, how can you be prepared? Well, the answer is easier and more obvious than you think. The first step to being prepared is mastering your craft or skill. Learn everything there is to know about your skill and spend your time mastering it while everyone else is resting. When you know what you are doing, regardless of the circumstances, you will always have the freedom to act on your instinct. Instead of scrambling at the last moment to determine what's to be done, you will have all the required skills and knowledge needed to make a good decision.

Understand Your True Self

Understanding your true self is important if you want to become unstoppable. If you don't like what you're doing or you are not concentrating on the things that matter or are important to you, you are essentially wasting the available resources. This also increases frustration and breeds dissatisfaction. If you want to become unstoppable and relentless, you must do what you like. If you enjoy your job, the chances of performing it effectively and efficiently improve. Ensure that all the decisions you make are in tune with your core values. Honesty, respect, love, passion, understanding, compassion, punctuality, etc., are examples of core values. Take some time for self-reflection and make a note of your core values. Use these values as guidelines for decision-making. When you do this, the quality of your life automatically improves because you are living according to your core values. When you are living life on your own terms, satisfaction, self-respect, and self-confidence increase.

Avoid External Motivations

We are all constantly motivated by different factors in life. The most common factor is money. Apart from money, other factors such as appreciation, the feeling of being accepted by others, or anything else along these lines are all external sources of motivation. The problem with external motivation is, it doesn't add anything to your life. We all want to have nice things and that is perfectly alright. Money can be a motivating factor, but it shouldn't be the only motivating factor. The problem with external motivation is, the urge to keep improving yourself or doing better goes away when the external source goes away. This is why you must ensure that motivation always stems from within. Your desire to become better, do better and become the best version of yourself is the best motivating factor. When this need comes from within, you will be comfortable pushing your personal limits and trying to do your best whenever possible.

Learn to be in Control

Most of us are reactive instead of proactive. This is because we feel everything that happens in our life is beyond our control. Regardless of how dire a situation seems, you always have a choice. You have the power to ensure you are in control. Unless you consciously give this control away, no one can take it from you. When you feel more in control of yourself and your habits, it becomes easier to stay in the zone needed to become unstoppable. Instead of reacting and acting on impulses, you learn to respond and make the most of the hand you are dealt. When you do things because you want to and not because you're forced to or because you believe you have to, productivity increases. As mentioned, if the factors motivating you are internal, the desire to keep going is intensified.

Don't be Satisfied

Satisfaction often results in complacency. Complacency doesn't amount to growth. When you become complacent in life, you start feeling content with whatever you have. If you are comfortable within the same space, there is no scope for growth and development. How can you become unstoppable if you don't venture beyond your comfort level? Satisfaction is usually associated with feeling comfortable in whatever you are doing or the person you have become. If you want to become unstoppable, ensure that testing your personal limits is your goal. It's not about achieving an objective or reaching a destination. Instead, it's about pushing yourself to see how far you can go.

Some believe this is similar to being ungrateful. If you take a moment, there is a slight difference here. Not being satisfied with whatever you are doing doesn't mean you are not grateful for all the good you have. Count your blessings while looking for different avenues to grow and develop. Avoid lingering too long at the table of success, because the only way you can learn to enjoy your next meal is if you get hungry.

Stress is Good

Stress can be good and bad. All that matters is how you respond to it. Holding yourself accountable, pushing yourself to do better, and increasing the pressure on yourself are simple ways to make stress work for you. This little added pressure ensures you are doing your best in any given situation. When this stress goes away, complacency steps into the picture. So, don't let the pressure off. For instance, a water pipe will burst under excess pressure. On the other hand, unless carbon is exposed to extreme levels of pressure, it won't turn into a diamond. So, all that matters is how you use this pressure to push yourself to move ahead. Added stress ensures that you are always alert and active. You need to do this if you want to make the most of all the opportunities available to you.

Make Others Compete with You

It was previously mentioned that most of us are often competing with others. If you constantly check how others are doing and fixate on everything absent in your life, you aren't working on improving yourself. Instead, you're simply trying to live a life that seems to be working for others. You should never compete with others because no two individuals are truly alike. What might work and make sense to others doesn't have to necessarily make sense to you. Understand what you desire and start working toward it. Instead of competing with others, make them want to compete with you. Stay true to yourself and be in your authentic zone. Ignore all the external noise and instead focus inward.

Don't be Scared of Failure

The fear of failure is quite real. When left unregulated, this fear can prevent you from taking any action. It's important to understand that success and failure go hand in hand. You cannot achieve success without facing failure. Failure also teaches you important life lessons which make success much sweeter. Don't hesitate to step outside your comfort zone because you are worried about failing. Unless you try, you will not know for sure. Even failure teaches us different lessons. The only factor that matters is whether you are willing to learn from them or not. If you believe failure is the end of the road, you are in trouble. Instead, if you think of it as a learning opportunity, you can move ahead. Remember, anything that doesn't kill you only makes you stronger. Chances are, there would have been circumstances in the past you thought you couldn't overcome. Well, here you are today. Use this as the motivation to keep going.

Always Learn

Never stop learning. It is highly unlikely that you know everything there is about a given topic. There will always be something you need to learn. Become a sponge and start absorbing all the information that comes your way. Be a lifelong student. If you want to become the best at anything, keep an open mind and keep learning. Don't stop honing and improving your skills and knowledge. This is the price you need to pay to become unstoppable. When everyone else is busy entertaining themselves, keep learning and pushing your boundaries to move ahead.

Own Your Mistakes

Making mistakes is not only common, but should be expected. This is also a part of life. Our mistakes give us a valuable opportunity to learn and grow. Every mistake, regardless of how damaging it is, is a learning opportunity. Once again, it depends on your perspective. Don't shy away from making mistakes. Similarly, don't hesitate to own your mistakes. Instead of blaming others and circumstances, look at what went wrong. If you are to be blamed, accept the responsibility. It takes a lot of self-confidence and self-esteem to accept mistakes. Own your mistakes, learn your lessons and avoid repeating them in the future.

Handling Success

Your attitude matters a lot in life. How you deal with failures is as important as how you deal with success. If you let success get to your head or become complacent after achieving it, it is not true success. Use your success to refuel your motivation to keep moving ahead. Don't let it become an overpowering external noise that prevents you from seeing all the other opportunities that come your way. Some believe success is the end of the journey. Well, it isn't. Success is a pit stop so treat it like one. There is a lot more to life than success. If you have achieved one goal, move on to the next one.

Don't let your success make it seem like certain things are beneath you. To achieve any goal, you need to start all over again; don't hesitate to do the grunt work.

Strengthen Your Mentality

Mental resilience and its power cannot be discounted or ignored. Resilience is the ability to bounce back from challenges and keep going despite all the obstacles that come your way. Keep nurturing your resilience because life will not be easy. True winners are the ones who keep going when everyone else gives up. This is what sets them apart from the rest. Even when situations aren't comfortable, make your peace with it. To do this, you need to become mentally strong. Mental resilience gives you the strength needed to face challenges instead of crumbling under pressure. Your thoughts are incredibly powerful because they influence every action you perform.

Let Your Work Speak

Your words amount to nothing without any action to back them. All unstoppable people are aware of this. Results convey more than your words can. Ensure that any work you do offers high value, is not easy to replicate, and is rare. On the other hand, any work that is quite common, low in value, and easily replicable is shallow; this is something anyone can do. The results of the work you do should be such that they cannot be ignored. Let your work speak for itself!

Confidence Matters

Self-confidence is the most powerful tool in your arsenal. It is the belief in your abilities and skills. It is knowing that you are equipped to deal with any problem instead of giving up. When you are confident, it becomes easier to deal with challenges and bounce back from setbacks. Self-confidence determines the size of challenges you undertake, how you will deal with setbacks, and the likelihood of attaining success. If you lack self-confidence, chances of success automatically reduce. Self-confidence gives you the internal strength needed to take on challenges in stride without worrying about failure.

Knowing you can do this colors your attitude with optimism.

Learn to Let Go

Forgiveness is an important life skill. It is not about proving yourself right or others wrong. It is not about justice. Instead, it's the simple act of letting go. It's about letting the past stay in the past. Forgiveness is needed for improving your emotional and mental health. It's also important for establishing healthy and meaningful relationships in life. When it comes to forgiveness, it's important to let go. That said, don't forget. When you learn to forgive, you are letting go of all unnecessary mental and emotional baggage that was holding you back. If you have been wronged by others, forgive them, but don't forget. Always learn your lessons in life and move on. If not, life has a funny way of teaching you the same lesson again.

Company Matters

The company you keep matters a lot in life. If you are surrounded by naysayers and pessimists, their pessimism will rub off on you sooner or later. Similarly, surrounding yourself with like-minded, positive, ambitious, and motivated people will have a positive effect on your psyche. The next time you meet someone, start paying attention to how you feel. There will be some who make you happy while others drain your energy. There will be some who motivate and encourage you to do better while others pull you down. Remember, you don't have space for any negativity in your life. Any relationship that does not add any meaning or value to your life isn't worth having. So, be around people who encourage you to work toward a better future. Be with those who push you to be better. Those who bring out the best in you are the ones worth holding onto.

Establishing Clear Goals

Establishing goals is crucial in all aspects of life. Regardless of whether it's your personal or professional life, you cannot make any progress without goals. Many don't think about it but establishing goals by itself is an important process. Your chances of success and whether you can achieve the goals or not depends on the goals you have set. When it comes to goal setting, ensure the goals are SMART. This implies they should be

S - small

M - measurable

A- attainable

R - relevant

T - time-bound

Even if one of these elements is missing, achieving it becomes impossible. In such instances, you are setting yourself up for failure.

While establishing goals, ensure that you believe in your goal. If not, the chances of attaining it reduces. The goal should be set in such a manner that you have a reason for attaining it and this reason should be strong enough to overcome any challenges, setbacks, or obstacles you face.

Elegance in Simplicity

Simplicity is elegant. If you want to get ahead and become successful, stop complicated things. Things become problematic because we overcomplicate them. Simplicity is not only elegant but is sophisticated too. Usually, the problem is that most of the challenges we face have simple solutions. If you start thinking about anything, you will realize that different factors, variables, and components result in complications. The more you think, the more complicated it all gets. Instead, try to look for simple solutions because they are often more effective than complicated ones.

Responding Immediately

Learning to respond immediately in any situation is an essential life skill. A response is not the same as a reaction. When you're reacting, you're not taking the time required to think the action through. While responding, you are thinking things through and taking action as well. Anticipating an event in this extremely dynamic world isn't easy. However, preparing yourself for different scenarios is easy. To become unstoppable, you need to learn to anticipate different events. Regardless of whether it's a positive or negative event, train yourself to respond immediately. Don't question yourself, don't overanalyze, and stop stalling. Instead, simply act. Until you take action, how you deal with the scenario is nothing more than a hypothetical situation in your head. When you take action, you get a chance to decide whether you are on the right course or not. You can make adjustments accordingly.

Don't be Jealous

Jealousy not only breeds contempt but increases dissatisfaction. When you constantly compare yourself with others or are jealous about how others are doing, it does not add any value or meaning to your life. Instead, you're simply wasting your time and mental resources focusing on others. Remember, if someone else succeeds, it doesn't mean you have failed. Similarly, more for others doesn't mean less for you. Learning to celebrate others' victories is a sign of self-confidence. It's a sign of internal strength and character. You don't have to be jealous or envious of their accomplishments. Others' successes and failures have nothing to do with you. The only person you are in control of is yourself. You are not someone else and therefore, comparing yourself to them is unfair. You have attributes, skills, and talents. Learn to make the most of your skills instead of becoming jealous that others seem to be better than you. If you want anything, remember, life has given you everything needed to make it happen.

Take a Shot

Letting go of the fear of failure is quite liberating. It gives you the motivation and confidence required to keep going regardless of the consequences. When you stop worrying about the outcomes and instead, just work on any opportunity that comes your way, your chances of success automatically increase. Life gives you different opportunities to take different shots. Whenever you don't take a shot, you are losing out on something. If you want to become unstoppable, you just need to take the shot. It doesn't matter whether you feel ready or not. It doesn't matter whether it's convenient or not. After all, life is about learning and growing.

Concentrate on the Efforts

One mistake many of us make is we concentrate on the results more than the efforts involved. When you start focusing only on the result, it increases frustration and can cause dissatisfaction. Don't get so caught up in the result of the success you desire that you forget about the efforts involved. If you don't make any effort, you cannot get the desired results. Don't make the mistake of riding the wave of your previous success to achieve success in the future. Instead, concentrate on all the effort that helped you achieve success the first time around. There are no shortcuts to success and don't forget this simple truth.

Push Yourself

The goals you establish should push you out of your comfort zone. Do you remember the saying "aim for the stars and you will land on the moon?" That's precisely how your goals should be established. Any goal that exceeds your existing capabilities will push you to improve yourself. If you keep working on yourself, you will become unstoppable. Instead of wishing things were easier, concentrate on making yourself better to become unstoppable.

Take Time to Recover

Never overlook the importance of taking the time needed to rest and rejuvenate. You are not a tireless machine so stop treating your body like one. Unless you take time to recover, you cannot function effectively and efficiently.

Engaging in meaningful work is better than being busy all the time. Being busy is not synonymous with producing results. When you take some time off, it gives you a chance to recover. It helps put things in perspective and ensures you are working in the right direction. Working effectively and efficiently is like exercising. Unless you take breaks between sets, you cannot improve your stamina, strength, or endurance. There are different ways to take breaks. Whether it's cooking, listening to music, or engaging in any of your hobbies, spend some time doing something you love. The break needs to be meaningful and rejuvenating. After you have rested and recovered, your body and mind will function as intended.

Stop Waiting

Most of us tend to wait until the moment is right to get started. We are waiting for the right circumstances, or until we are motivated enough to start. Well, this is counterintuitive to productivity. Unless you start, you cannot get anything done. Instead of waiting for the right circumstances or conditions, simply take the first step. Some people have brilliant ideas, but never implement them because they want to wait until they feel secure or comfortable. Well, this doesn't happen. Once you take the first step, it builds momentum that propels you forward. So, stop waiting and start doing.

Rule About Permission

If you need permission to do something, chances are you probably shouldn't do it. If you want to do something, permission doesn't matter. Always remember this whenever you want to do something different. Instead of chasing whatever works for others, concentrate on doing what you want to and your reasons for it. This is the only way to strike gold. Stop following plans that worked for others. Others' successes shouldn't be your yardstick for doing well in life.

There are No Exceptions

If you want to become unstoppable, remember there are no exceptions. For instance, if you are shifting to a healthier lifestyle, it takes consistency, a conscious effort, and deliberate action. Without consistency, you cannot get the desired result. It means you need to do things even when you don't want to. This is how you attain success. If you have started exercising, you need to exercise daily to reap the benefits it offers. Exercising for two days and taking a break from the new routine doesn't make any sense. So, ensure there are no exceptions. Ensure you're doing something productive daily. It's always small steps that add up to significant results.

You can become extraordinary, provided you want to.

Conclusion

Facing challenges is not only normal but is an unavoidable part of life. Life isn't just about success and happiness. Instead, it's about all the different experiences that are a result of things both good and bad. Every experience in your life is a learning opportunity. As long as you are willing to learn and grow, you will become unstoppable. Unfortunately, young women usually face more challenges than their male counterparts whether they're being crushed under societal expectations or struggling to make themselves be seen and heard in their personal and professional lives. Regardless of the events that take place, you have complete control over what you decide in every circumstance and situation. This choice is entirely yours. No one can take this power away from you unless you consciously give it away. You have the strength within to get past any challenges and reclaim your inner peace of mind. You can live up to your true potential.

If you want to achieve the impossible, you need to rise to all the challenges life throws your way. Rising up to challenges is an important skill because they are a part of life. You cannot avoid challenges and certain things should be expected. When faced with a challenge, how you deal with it is all that matters. Stop listening to your inner fears and instead, learn to stand up for yourself. You have what it takes to rise to any challenge that comes your way. You can overcome all challenges.

Promise yourself that there is always a way out. Regardless of how troubling or challenging the circumstances might seem right now, they are not permanent. Change is the only constant in life; remember this whenever you are dealing with challenging circumstances. There is always a way out and all you need to do is actively look for it. If you want to achieve greatness, you need to dream big. Don't shy away from dreaming big because you have the power to achieve the extraordinary. When you dream big, you are automatically setting the bar higher. It also helps create the positive attitude needed to get through life's challenges.

Nothing is impossible if you put your mind to it and believe you can do it. Work on creating a positive and gratitude-based mindset. Instead of fearing failure, use it as a stepping stone toward success. Success and failure are two sides of the same coin. By engaging in positive self-talk and making small moves, you can transform yourself. When you do this, you are living up to your full potential. Never let anyone put you down or talk down to you. You are unique, and extremely strong the way you are. Don't change yourself for others. Don't do anything that you don't want to. Always remember that success isn't final and therefore, it shouldn't become the basis for your self-worth. Failure is not fatal as long as you dare to keep going. Learn your lessons from the mistakes you made. Accept all challenges that come your way and take them in a positive stride. While you do all this, do not forget about yourself in the process. Ensure that you are living the life you desire.

While dealing with the different challenges you face in life, chances are that self-love often takes a backseat. If you truly want to become unstoppable and achieve the impossible while realizing your potential, you need to start taking care of yourself. Women are expected to play the role of nurturer. Unfortunately, when they are taking care of so many responsibilities, they are left with nothing for themselves. All the love and compassion usually reserved for others should be directed toward yourself first. Understand that the true key to happiness and love lies in your hands. True happiness always stems from within and do not look for it elsewhere. When you are happy on the inside, no one else can take it away from you. Similarly, you need to love and accept yourself unconditionally. When you do this, your self-confidence and self-esteem automatically increase. This, in turn, increases the chances of success.

Never, ever underestimate your capability. If you want to live your life like a champion, you mustn't give up. Always remember that life might not be easy but you have the power to write your own destiny. You have the power to go from being undervalued to becoming unstoppable and truly extraordinary. All you need to do is make certain simple changes to your daily routine; whether it's cultivating an attitude of positivity or letting go of self-doubt.

Now is the time to take action. You need to get out there and start implementing the simple and practical suggestions given in this book to discover your true potential! If you enjoyed reading this book, please take a couple of minutes and leave a review about it on Amazon. I'm sure that your feedback and personal experience will help others out there!

References

All images courtesy of Pixabay - Pixabay. (2018). Pixabay. Pixabay.com. https://pixabay.com/

5 tips to develop an ACTION MINDSET and beat procrastination – Thrive at Work. (n.d.). Https://thriveatwork.com.au/5-tips-to-develop-an-action-mindset-and-beat-procrastination/

10 Ways How to Overcome Challenges Life Throws at You. (2020, March 30). University of the People. https://www.uopeople.edu/blog/10-ways-how-to-overcome-challenges/

12 Empowering Lessons About Failure. (2017, August 17). SUCCESS. Https://www.success.com/12-empowering-lessons-about-failure/

Alpert, J. (2015, October 8). How You Can
        Make the Impossible Possible.
        Inc.com.
        Https://www.inc.com/jonathan-
        alpert/how-to-make-the-impossible-
        possible.html

Battles, Dr. M. (2016, December 19). 15
        Ways to Practice Positive Self-Talk
        for Success. Lifehack; Lifehack.
        https://www.lifehack.org/504756/sel
        f-talk-determines-your-success-15-
        tips

Bueso, S. (2018, January 6). How to Rise to
        Challenges Successfully. Silvia
        Bueso.
        Https://silviabueso.com/how-to-
        rise-to-challenges-successfully/

Burnford, J. (2019, June 30). Limiting
        Beliefs: What Are They and How
        Can You Overcome Them? Forbes.
        Https://www.forbes.com/sites/joybu

rnford/2019/01/30/limiting-beliefs-what-are-they-and-how-can-you-overcome-them/?Sh=608167f46303

Chen, Y. (2019, May 20). Understand Your Worth – How You Value Yourself | Ye Chen. Https://ye-chen.com/understand-your-worth-how-you-value-yourself/

Daskal, L. (2018, March 26). 10 Things to Remember When You Are Feeling Stuck. Inc.com. Https://www.inc.com/lolly-daskal/10-things-to-remember-when-you-are-feeling-stuck.html

Denning, T. (2018, May 22). How To Understand Your True Value And Never Sell Yourself Short Again. Medium. Https://medium.com/the-mission/how-to-understand-your-true-value-and-never-sell-yourself-short-again-66d527197608

Deschene, L. (2010, January 11). 7 Ways to Get Past Tough Situations Quickly. Tiny Buddha. https://tinybuddha.com/blog/7-ways-to-get-past-tough-situations-quickly/

Ezeanu, E. (2013, December 4). 7 Things to Remember When Going Through Tough Times in Life. Lifehack. https://www.lifehack.org/articles/productivity/7-things-people-forget-when-they-are-down-and-going-through-the-tough-times-life.html

Fenton, R. (2019, April 15). Here Are Some Tips on How Enduring Failure Is the Secret for Success. The Balance Small Business. Https://www.thebalancesmb.com/turning-failure-into-success-2948457

Hardy, B. (2017, August 31). 30 Behaviors That Will Make You Unstoppable.

Thriveglobal.in.
Https://thriveglobal.in/stories/30-
behaviors-that-will-make-you-
unstoppable/

Ho, L. (2007, May 28). Why You Have the
Fear of Failure (And How to
Conquer It Step-By-Step). Lifehack;
Lifehack.
https://www.lifehack.org/articles/lif
ehack/how-fear-of-failure-destroys-
success.html

Houlis, A. (n.d.). 10 Strategies for
Thinking outside the Box That Will
Impress Your Boss.
Fairygodboss.com.
Https://fairygodboss.com/career-
topics/think-outside-the-box

Hurst, K. (2016, July 29). 10 Things to
Remember When You're Feeling
Stuck In Life. The Law of Attraction.
Https://www.thelawofattraction.co

m/10-things-remember-youre-
feeling-stuck-life/

Kashyap, V. (n.d.). How to set your mind
to believe you can achieve the
impossible. Www.linkedin.com.
Https://www.linkedin.com/pulse/ho
w-set-your-mind-believe-you-can-
achieve-impossible-vartika-kashyap

Koulopoulos, T. (2018, August 5). Four
Ways to Overcome the Impossible.
Disruptor League.
Https://www.disruptorleague.com/
blog/2018/08/05/four-ways-to-
overcome-the-impossible/

Mazzocchi, A. (2013, April 11). 14
Powerful Ways to Be Fearless.
Lifehack.
Https://www.lifehack.org/articles/co
mmunication/14-ways-to-be-
fearless.html

Murphy Jr, B. (2014, March 24). 17 Things Extraordinary People Do Every Day. Inc.com. Https://www.inc.com/bill-murphy-jr/17-things-extraordinary-people-do-every-day.html

Sasson, R. (2012, June 15). Don't Allow People and Circumstances Control Your Life. Https://www.successconsciousness.com/blog/personal-development/dont-allow-people-and-circumstances-control-your-life/

Skye, E. (2015, July 10). How To Dream Big, Set Goals And Achieve What You Want. Women's Running. Https://www.womensrunning.com/training/how-to-dream-big-set-goals-and-achieve-what-you-want/

Stewart, A. R. (2017, November 17). 13 Habits of Self-Love Every Woman Should Adopt. Healthline. Https://www.healthline.com/health/13-self-love-habits-every-woman-needs-to-have#1.-Stop-comparing-yourself-to-others

Verma, D. (2021, May 24). 7 Ways to Stop Letting Other People Affect You - Life, Cosmopolitan India. Cosmopolitan India. Https://www.cosmopolitan.in/life/features/a24178/7-ways-stop-letting-other-people-affect-you

www.ingramcontent.com/pod-product-compliance
Lightning Source LLC
Chambersburg PA
CBHW070713130626
46553CB00005B/1974